Learning IBM Bluemix

Demystify application development on cloud platform by leveraging the power of IBM Bluemix

Sreelatha Sankaranarayanan

BIRMINGHAM - MUMBAI

Learning IBM Bluemix

First published: October 2016

Production reference: 1171016

Published by Packt Publishing Ltd.

Livery Place

35 Livery Street

Birmingham B3 2PB, UK.

ISBN 978-1-78588-774-1

www.packtpub.com

Credits

Authors

Sreelatha Sankaranarayanan

Reviewers

Mohan P Annamalai

Commissioning Editor

Pratik Shah

Acquisition Editor

Nitin Dasan

Content Development Editor

Priyanka Mehta

Technical Editors

Dhiraj Chandanshive

Copy Editor

Safis Editing

Project Coordinator

Izzat Contractor

Proofreader

Safis Editing

Indexer

Tejal Daruwale Soni

Production Coordinator

Shraddha Falebhai

Cover Work

Shraddha Falebhai

About the Author

Sreelatha Sankaranarayanan has close to 16 years of experience in software engineering. She has been with Phoenix Global Solutions (now Tata Consultancy Services) for close to 2.5 years. She is currently with IBM India and has been with them for the last 13.5 years. During her career, she has been part of product development, support, and test teams, primarily working on enterprise middleware products. In her most recent role, she was responsible for evangelizing IBM's cloud platform as-a-service, Bluemix, and has worked with System Integrators, academia, and IBM partners to enable and support them with the adoption of IBM's cloud platform as-a-service, Bluemix. She has coauthored a redbook entitled *B2B Solutions using WebSphere Partner Gateway v6.0*, authored some developerWorks articles, and some blog posts on the Mobile Enterprise Application Platform (MEAP), Internet of Things (IoT), and cloud platform as-a-service (Bluemix). You can find her on Twitter at `@sreelathas` and on LinkedIn at `https://in.linkedin.com/in/sreelathas`.

I thank Packt Publishing and Nitin Dasan for providing me with the opportunity and support to author this book. Special mention to the editorial reviewer, Priyanka Mehta, and the technical reviewer, Mohan P Annamalai (IBM), who have worked to refine each of the chapters in this book. We hope that you enjoy and learn as much as we, as author and reviewers, have enjoyed and learned putting this book together.

About the Reviewer

Mohan P Annamalai is a senior manager at IBM India Private Ltd, with 16 years of experience in the IT industry. He is currently responsible for driving the development efforts for Mobile Foundation Service on Bluemix. Prior to this, he successfully managed the efforts for setting up the IBM Push Notifications service on Bluemix. He was also responsible for driving IBM Bluemix eco system from India Software Labs in the year 2014. In this role, he worked with key IBM system integrators to gain interest on Bluemix. In his role as the IBM Bluemix program manager, he played a pivotal role in gaining mind share for IBM Bluemix among the developers and students in India. Apart from mobile and cloud, Mohan led the delivery of the analytics service component to power analytics in couple of key IBM solutions. He has also worked for Satyam Computer Services Limited. He started his career as a J2EE developer in connectivity and integration products and became a development manager in the same space.

www.PacktPub.com

For support files and downloads related to your book, please visit www.PacktPub.com.

eBooks, discount offers, and more

Did you know that Packt offers eBook versions of every book published, with PDF and ePub files available? You can upgrade to the eBook version at www.PacktPub.com and as a print book customer, you are entitled to a discount on the eBook copy. Get in touch with us at customercare@packtpub.com for more details.

At www.PacktPub.com, you can also read a collection of free technical articles, sign up for a range of free newsletters and receive exclusive discounts and offers on Packt books and eBooks.

https://www2.packtpub.com/books/subscription/packtlib

Do you need instant solutions to your IT questions? PacktLib is Packt's online digital book library. Here, you can search, access, and read Packt's entire library of books.

Why subscribe?

- Fully searchable across every book published by Packt
- Copy and paste, print, and bookmark content
- On demand and accessible via a web browser

Free access for Packt account holders

Get notified! Find out when new books are published by following @PacktEnterprise on Twitter or the Packt Enterprise Facebook page.

Table of Contents

Preface

Cloud computing is an important transformative force defining the technology landscape today. Cloud computing has changed the way technology can be built and used for business, industry, governance, academia, and the like. Cloud technology is also considered as a key enabler to building innovations that define newer markets. Given the importance and relevance of this space, it is but natural to consider talking about one such cloud platform called Bluemix, which is a **platform as-a-service** (**PaaS**) offering from IBM.

This book is an attempt to compile illustrative descriptions for the different capabilities offered by Bluemix. The intended audience for this book is developers who are relatively new to the space of application development on a platform as-a-service environment. This book also serves to jumpstart developers who want to learn and use IBM Bluemix.

This book gives you the levers to understand Bluemix as a platform, learn how to use the value-added services on Bluemix, understand how to build, manage, and monitor applications on Bluemix, discover the options of deployment on Bluemix, and above all, witness the ease and the innovative approach to discover and cater to different types of use cases solving problems in varied categories.

This book is written in a simple, appealing, explanatory format with sufficient visual aids in the form of screenshots so that it is easy to follow even for those of you who are not very technical. As the author of this book, I am certain that you will experience a learning that you can build upon later; you will find that this provides an apt landing platform from where you are equipped to take the plunge.

What this book covers

Chapter 1, *Saying Hello to IBM Bluemix,* covers cloud computing and cloud service delivery models, and then lets us take a look at what Bluemix is. It also covers the different ways in which the platform is offered, along with an introduction to the IBM Bluemix public offering.

Chapter 2, *Building and Deploying Your First Hello World Application on Bluemix*, introduces you to application building on IBM Bluemix. You will learn how to build a simple application on Bluemix and deploy and run it.

Chapter 3, *Extending an Application and Configuring for Continuous Delivery Using DevOps Services*, teaches you how to extend existing applications on Bluemix to build additional functionality using some of the value-added services on Bluemix; this is illustrated along with a sample application.

Chapter 4, *Leveraging On-Premise Software for Applications on Bluemix*, demonstrates a very important aspect of modern application building environment, called hybrid cloud. We will see how on-premise or local software or applications can be leveraged to integrate with newer applications that are to be deployed on public cloud infrastructure.

Chapter 5, *Scaling Applications in Bluemix*, introduces you to application scaling. You will learn about the scaling options supported on Bluemix: manual and auto-scaling.

Chapter 6, *Monitoring and Management in Bluemix*, discusses the different services that can be used to monitor and manage applications. You will learn to work with the Monitoring and Analytics service for a web application deployed on Bluemix. Additionally, the chapter introduces readers to NewRelic, which is a third-party service on Bluemix.

Chapter 7, *Compute Options on Bluemix*, covers the different compute options available on Bluemix, such as containers, Cloud Foundry applications, virtual servers, and Open Whisk.

Chapter 8, *Security Services on Bluemix*, talks about the security services available on Bluemix and elaborates two of the available security services in Bluemix. You will learn how to offload the web application authentication functionality to the Single Sign On service on Bluemix.

Chapter 9, *Microservices-based Application Development on Bluemix*, talks about an architecture pattern for application development on the cloud, called the Microservices architecture pattern. You will also learn how to use Bluemix and services on Bluemix to build and deploy applications that employ the microservices architecture.

Chapter 10, *Mobile Application Development on Bluemix*, introduces you to services offered on Bluemix that are specifically for mobile application development. You will learn how to use some of these services to build a simple mobile catalog application.

What you need for this book

Here's what you require for this book:

- Cloud Foundry CLI (the latest version available)
- Eclipse IDE (v4.4 or later)

Who this book is for

This book is aimed at developers seeking to learn application development and deployment methods on IBM Bluemix. A basic knowledge of Java and Node.js is assumed.

Conventions

In this book, you will find a number of text styles that distinguish between different kinds of information. Here are some examples of these styles and an explanation of their meaning. Code words in text, database table names, folder names, filenames, file extensions, pathnames, dummy URLs, user input, and Twitter handles are shown as follows: "You will notice that the deployable artifact for your application is the `webApp.war` file."

A block of code is set as follows:

```
@Override
protected void init(VaadinRequest vaadinRequest) {
  Responsive.makeResponsive(this);
  setLocale(vaadinRequest.getLocale());
  getPage().setTitle("MyVaadinApp");
  showMainView();
}
```

New terms and important words are shown in bold. Words that you see on the screen, for example, in menus or dialog boxes, appear in the text like this: "Enter your LinkedIn credentials and click **Allow access**."

 Warnings or important notes appear in a box like this.

Tips and tricks appear like this.

Reader feedback

Feedback from our readers is always welcome. Let us know what you think about this book—what you liked or disliked. Reader feedback is important for us as it helps us develop titles that you will really get the most out of.

To send us general feedback, simply e-mail feedback@packtpub.com, and mention the book's title in the subject of your message.

If there is a topic that you have expertise in and you are interested in either writing or contributing to a book, see our author guide at www.packtpub.com/authors.

Customer support

Now that you are the proud owner of a Packt book, we have a number of things to help you to get the most from your purchase.

Downloading the example code

You can download the example code files for this book from your account at http://www.packtpub.com. If you purchased this book elsewhere, you can visit http://www.packtpub.com/support and register to have the files e-mailed directly to you.

You can download the code files by following these steps:

1. Log in or register to our website using your e-mail address and password.
2. Hover the mouse pointer on the **SUPPORT** tab at the top.
3. Click on **Code Downloads & Errata**.
4. Enter the name of the book in the **Search** box.
5. Select the book for which you're looking to download the code files.
6. Choose from the drop-down menu where you purchased this book from.
7. Click on **Code Download**.

You can also download the code files by clicking on the **Code Files** button on the book's webpage at the Packt Publishing website. This page can be accessed by entering the book's name in the Search box. Please note that you need to be logged in to your Packt account.

Once the file is downloaded, please make sure that you unzip or extract the folder using the latest version of:

- WinRAR / 7-Zip for Windows
- Zipeg / iZip / UnRarX for Mac
- 7-Zip / PeaZip for Linux

The code bundle for the book is also hosted on GitHub at `https://github.com/PacktPubl ishing/LearningIBMBluemix`. We also have other code bundles from our rich catalog of books and videos available at `https://github.com/PacktPublishing/`. Check them out!

Downloading the color images of this book

We also provide you with a PDF file that has color images of the screenshots/diagrams used in this book. The color images will help you better understand the changes in the output. You can download this file from `http://www.packtpub.com/sites/default/files/downloads/LearningIBMBluemix_ColorI mages.pdf`.

Errata

Although we have taken every care to ensure the accuracy of our content, mistakes do happen. If you find a mistake in one of our books—maybe a mistake in the text or the code—we would be grateful if you could report this to us. By doing so, you can save other readers from frustration and help us improve subsequent versions of this book. If you find any errata, please report them by visiting `http://www.packtpub.com/submit-errata`, selecting your book, clicking on the Errata Submission Form link, and entering the details of your errata. Once your errata are verified, your submission will be accepted and the errata will be uploaded to our website or added to any list of existing errata under the Errata section of that title.

To view the previously submitted errata, go to `https://www.packtpub.com/books/conten t/support` and enter the name of the book in the search field. The required information will appear under the Errata section.

Piracy

Piracy of copyrighted material on the Internet is an ongoing problem across all media. At Packt, we take the protection of our copyright and licenses very seriously. If you come across any illegal copies of our works in any form on the Internet, please provide us with the location address or website name immediately so that we can pursue a remedy.

Please contact us at copyright@packtpub.com with a link to the suspected pirated material.

We appreciate your help in protecting our authors and our ability to bring you valuable content.

Questions

If you have a problem with any aspect of this book, you can contact us at questions@packtpub.com, and we will do our best to address the problem.

1
Saying Hello to IBM Bluemix

Ready to rock with IBM Bluemix? Not yet? Don't fret; we are here to take you through your exciting journey to embrace the whole new paradigm of application development on cloud.

Before we take the plunge, let us equip ourselves with an understanding of some of the concepts that are at the periphery but that are essential to build your know-how of IBM Bluemix.

Heard of cloud computing? No? Well, we highly recommend you have a basic understanding of what cloud computing is at this point, before we can move forward. If we were to define it in simple terms, cloud computing is the method of creating a pool of resources (compute, storage, and network) and offering it through a simple portal that allows users to request the resources they want and get them provisioned in minutes, all this at a cost that is charged against the actual usage metrics of the resources or on a period-based consumption model.

Did you get it? No? Let us simplify it further.

Think of resources as compute, storage, and networking.

Now think of these resources being pooled and shared in a data center by what we call **cloud service provider** or **CSP**.

As a user, you will need a certain compute, storage, and networking capacity to host your application. In a non-traditional cloud world, you would go to the URL of the CSP, which will take you to the self-service portal of his service. Through this portal, you will be able to look at the available resources offered by the CSP, look at the costs at which each of them is offered, and will also be able to request a combination of resources based on your requirements. This custom compute capacity will be provisioned to you inside your tenancy or account with the CSP cloud offering. You will then be able to access and work with your resources through public Internet calls. This is a typical scenario of using cloud computing on a public cloud. By public cloud, what is meant is that the resources are shared and accessible by anyone on the public Internet, once they have a tenancy or account established within the cloud offering. Tenancy will assure resource isolation between tenants. Public cloud platforms are a popular way to explain the concept of cloud computing; however, there are private and hybrid flavors of cloud computing that CSPs provide. We shall discuss this further along in this chapter.

In this chapter, we will be looking at the following topics:

- Understanding cloud service delivery models
- Getting a step closer to understanding IBM Bluemix
- Understanding Bluemix architecture
- Familiarizing with Bluemix deployment models
- Getting an account on public Bluemix
- Understanding the Bluemix dashboard

Understanding cloud service delivery models

Having understood the cloud computing model, let us graduate ourselves to the next level, where we will get an understanding of the three different service delivery models in cloud, which is to say in simple words, what can I get from a CSP?

To understand the cloud service delivery models, we need to focus on what we need from a cloud platform and what is provided to us by a cloud service provider; together, they define the as-a-service paradigm of the cloud or the cloud service delivery model.

What do we mean by as-a-service? As-a-service is a new business model, where the consumer does not have to buy a product or solution in its entirety for lifetime use. In the as-a-service model, a consumer buys the rights to use a product or solution for a defined period, in its entirety; the period can be renewed or continued based on the consumer's requirement. There is no lock-in or upfront huge investments needed in the as-a-service model. Applied to IT, this as-a-service model is cost viable for most small to mid-size organizations and start-ups. This has allowed for exploitation of software solutions to bring in business transformation through rapidly developed ubiquitous and innovative applications.

Let us take a look at what the cloud service delivery models are. In the broad category, we have three cloud service delivery models; there have been other specific categories as well, but to discuss all service delivery models is outside the scope of this book. The three cloud service delivery models are as follows:

- **Infrastructure as-a-service** (**IaaS**)
- **Platform as-a-service** (**Paas**)
- **Software as-a-service** (**SaaS**)

The following figure shows a pictorial definition of each of the as-a-service models. IT within an enterprise consists of the nine broad layers of infrastructure components, such as networking, storage, servers and virtualization, and middleware; application infrastructure components such as operating system, and runtime; and a software stack of applications and data:

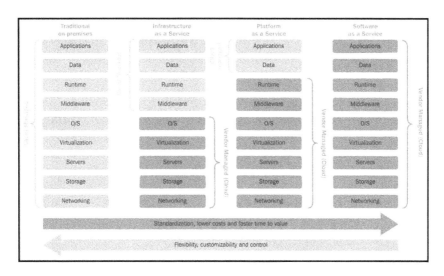

Cloud service delivery models

In a traditional on-premise environment, all the layers are procured, managed, and maintained by the consumer, who is typically an enterprise. If the consumer opts to not invest in infrastructure and instead leverage infrastructure provided as a service by a cloud service provider, then the consumer is operating in an infrastructure as-a-service model; the stack above the infrastructure components are still procured, managed, and maintained by him. This model is useful when there is a need for elasticity in infrastructure to support ever-changing business demands. This model absolves the consumer of being locked down by huge investments in infrastructure if he has to support a shrinkage in his needs. On the other hand, it also helps the consumer expand his IT in response to the increase in business need.

Taking this discussion to the next level, in the third stack from the figure, we see that in addition to the infrastructure components, we also see a model where the cloud service providers provide the application infrastructure components as a service along with the infrastructure components. This model is called platform as-a-service. Essentially, what this translates to is a multi-tenanted environment where development and deployment of applications can be done collaboratively with the support of value-added software products and solutions offered as a service on the same platform. This model is useful when the consumer wants an easy bring up and tear down development environment, where quick and dirty prototypes can be built. The prototypes can be graduated to a full-fledged production-ready application that is hosted and maintained on the same platform. Again, as with any other as-a-service model with PaaS too, the consumer is not vendor locked and is absolved of upfront huge license costs, when he is still evaluating technology, an exception to this would be when the customer brings his own license (BYOL) to use a specific software as-a-service on the PaaS.

Lastly, software as-a-service is a model where the entire application stack from the infrastructure components all the way up to the application and application data are vendor managed. The user is merely an end consumer of the software application.

As we move from a traditional, on-premise environment to a completely vendor managed software stack, the flexibility and customizability options with the consumer decreases; also, the control that the consumer will have on different layers of the stack decreases. However, the lower costs and speed and agility with faster time to value are achieved as we move from the traditional environments through the types of as-a-service models.

Getting a step closer to understanding IBM Bluemix

Bluemix is an open source Cloud Foundry-based platform as-a-service offering from IBM. Bluemix is not just a hosting of open source Cloud Foundry; Bluemix provides value additions such as:

- An intuitive dashboard to interact with the Cloud Foundry layer and to work with Bluemix
- A suite of enterprise middleware and software offered as services on Bluemix
- IBM support for the platform and IBM services
- Deployment models to choose from, such as public, dedicated, and local
- Rich IBM community business partners offering value added services
- Community support through the IBM developerWorks network

The following figure gives a high-level snapshot of what the Bluemix platform is composed of; Bluemix is not limited to what follows, but this figure gives a simplistic view of the components available on Bluemix for users to work with. Bluemix provides a rich and wide set of IBM software offered as managed services; these include services for application development and deployment known as DevOps services, services that enable hybrid applications to be developed and hosted through the use of integration services, cognitive services from Watson, Mobile services for mobile application development and management, data and analytics services to work with application data, and a host of runtime support for your applications, such as Java, NodeJS, Ruby, php, Python, Groovy, and so on:

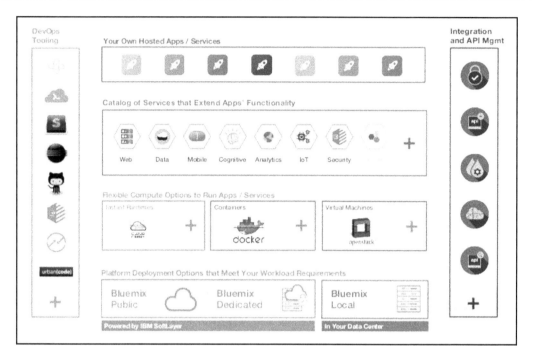

High-level view of what Bluemix offers

You will also see here in the figure that Bluemix offers different compute options for your applications, based on your needs. In addition to the Cloud Foundry-based applications, you can also deploy your applications and host them on Bluemix by using a Docker container or open stack-based virtual machines. IBM also has announced the IBM Open Whisk compute environment, which is ideal for applications that are event-based. To know more about the compute options in Bluemix, refer to `https://www.bluemix.net/docs/compute/index.html`.

Understanding the Bluemix architecture

Bluemix is a Cloud Foundry-based platform as-a-service offering from IBM. Cloud Foundry is the open source standard for PaaS. To understand in-depth details on cloud foundry internals, you can refer to `http://docs.cloudfoundry.org/`.

The following figure gives a high-level overview of Bluemix architecture. We will scope our discussion to the public deployment model of Bluemix; however, for dedicated and local Bluemix deployments (about which we shall learn more later in the chapter), the Bluemix internals based on Cloud Foundry architecture remain the same; what would change is the infrastructure on which Bluemix is hosted:

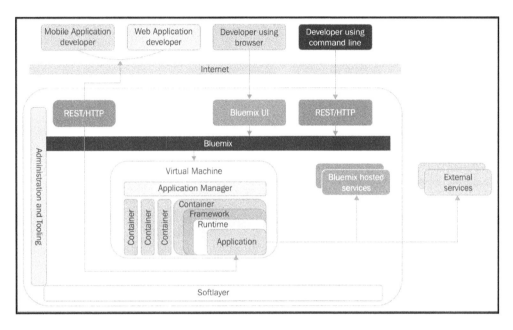

Bluemix high level overview

In the preceding figure, you can see that Bluemix is hosted on Softlayer infrastructure. An application hosted on Bluemix would run within the VM on Softlayer, each of the VMs will have resource isolation through containers, and each container will have the runtime and framework components necessary to run an application.

Applications on Bluemix are monitored for their health and managed by an application manager. Developers can use a browser or the cloud foundry command line client to work with Bluemix. The details on Bluemix UI are discussed in future sections of this chapter; we will also be discussing details on working with Bluemix using the cloud foundry command line in future chapters.

Bluemix catalog offers services that are hosted on Bluemix or those that run outside of it. Services are IBM provided, community-based, or third-party software or middleware that is offered from the Bluemix platform as-a-service, which is, in other words, ready-to-use software that is billed on a pay as you use model, without prior license purchase and so on.

Familiarizing yourself with Bluemix deployment models

Bluemix is offered as a service in three deployment models. They are as follows:

- Public Bluemix
- Dedicated Bluemix
- Local Bluemix

Public Bluemix

Bluemix is offered as a public multi-tenanted platform as-a-service offering. Public Bluemix is available currently in three datacenters (at the time of writing this book). Public Bluemix is great for startups, open community developers, freelance developers, students, and for specific requirements of small to medium or even large enterprises. This is a great platform for experimenting with technology, building the quick and dirty prototypes, and also, a platform for building and hosting business applications that are not stringent on regulatory and compliance requirements. As discussed in this chapter and for most of this book, we will be using public Bluemix, which can be accessed from `www.bluemix.net`.

Dedicated Bluemix

Unlike public Bluemix, dedicated Bluemix is hosted on a single tenanted dedicated Softlayer infrastructure. If you want a dedicated Bluemix setup, then the infrastructure underlying this dedicated Bluemix is also dedicated to you. The hardware is not shared with any other users. Dedicated Bluemix makes a hybrid environment possible, where you can leverage the advantages of cloud development along with the data from within your enterprise.

Dedicated Bluemix can be set up to sit within your enterprise VPN network and user identity management can be integrated to your enterprise identity management system. This will allow dedicated Bluemix to be a platform that is truly dedicated and customizable for your enterprise. Services on dedicated Bluemix can be customized based on what you really need, as opposed to out of the box catalog.

Dedicated Bluemix is suitable for application deployments that have greater security, regulatory, and compliance requirements. Also, in cases where there is a need to have greater control over audit data or application data, this kind of Bluemix deployment is suggested.

Apart from the regular Bluemix dashboard, dedicated Bluemix has what is called the admin console. This is an operations console that the administrators of the dedicated Bluemix environment within your organization can use to manage and administer the Bluemix platform within their enterprise. The functions that can be carried out using the admin console would be as follows:

- User administration
- Catalog management
- Organization administration
- View system/dedicated Bluemix updates or scheduled updates
- Monitor the usage of resources across the organizations within the dedicated Bluemix account
- Access and view reports and logs for activities on the environment

Another important aspect worth mentioning about dedicated Bluemix is the syndicated catalog. Dedicated Bluemix provides the ability for its users to use software services across their public or dedicated Bluemix environments. A single palette of services catalog is displayed to the dedicated Bluemix user, from where he can choose services that he would like to use for his application. Dedicated services are marked with a red icon on the top right, as shown in the following screenshot; the grayed-out service is one that is turned off or made unavailable for the given organization in the dedicated Bluemix through the admin console, which was discussed earlier. Services that are from public Bluemix syndicated to the dedicated Bluemix catalog are shown in a separate category of services and they do not have the red icon to the top right corner, as was the case with dedicated services.

The pricing and support models are also different from public Bluemix. To learn more about dedicated Bluemix you can refer to `http://www.ibm.com/cloud-computing/bluemix/dedicated/`.

Local Bluemix

Bluemix delivered as a service within the firewall boundaries of your enterprise on your infrastructure or within your datacenter is called local Bluemix. You can imagine it to be a private cloud offering a PaaS platform. The core Bluemix platform is the same across public, dedicated, or local.

Local Bluemix is typically useful where the sensitivity, privacy, and security needs of applications and application data is very stringent. An example would be government agencies or government bodies; they are usually governed by very strict regulatory and compliance standards and often would need hosting and operating environments that are mostly under their control.

The architecture of Bluemix local is given in detail at `http://www.ibm.com/cloud-computing/bluemix/local/imgs/the-architects-guide-to-bluemix-local.pdf`.

 The first step in your journey to learning Bluemix is to learn how to create your own account on IBM Bluemix.

Getting an account on public Bluemix

Creating an account on Bluemix would be the first step for you to get access to a variety of resources that you will use to create, deploy, and run your application. Throughout this book, we will use the public multi-tenanted offering of IBM Bluemix to work with. Let us learn on how to create your Bluemix account:

1. Ensure you have Internet connectivity, open your browser, and go to `www.bluemix.net`.
2. Click **SIGN UP**, as shown in the following screenshot:

3. You can sign up for a 30-day free trial of Bluemix. Once you click **SIGN UP**, you will be taken to the page as follows; a couple of things that you should pay attention to on this page are as follows:

    - You are providing information on this page to create an IBM ID; if you already have an IBM ID, created as part of your work with any other IBM products or offerings, then you can use it to log in to Bluemix. You can then skip the sign up step. If you do not have an IBM ID, then please follow the steps here to create one.

- By the sign up process, you are entitled to the 30-day free trial of IBM Bluemix. You will be able to log in to Bluemix and use all the resources on it for free during this trial period:

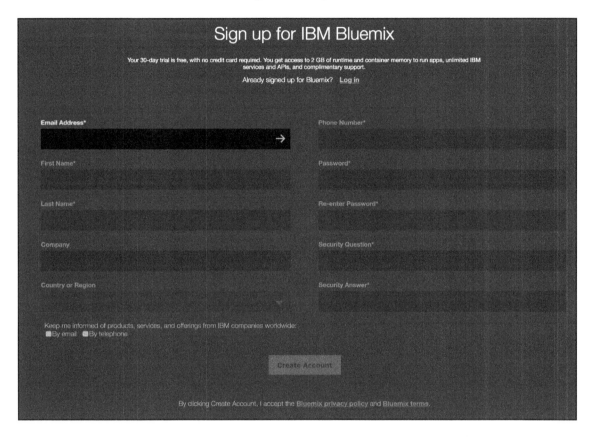

4. Provide your details in the fields shown in the **SIGN UP** screen and click **CREATE ACCCOUNT**. This will create your IBM ID and you will get further login information on your e-mail address that you have provided during sign up. Once you click **CREATE ACCOUNT**, you will see the following page on successful submission:

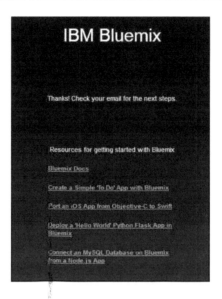

5. You will receive an e-mail, as shown in the following screenshot, for reference; you will need to first confirm your account by clicking the **Confirm your account** link. Once this is done, you can log in to www.bluemix.net using your newly created IBM ID and password. If you face any login-related issues, please log the problem with http://ibm.biz/bluemixsupport and the Bluemix support team will get in touch with you to fix the issue:

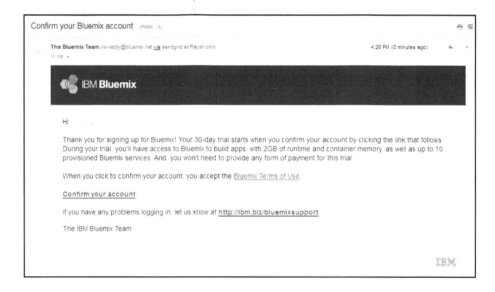

6. On confirming the account, by clicking the **Confirm your account** link, you will see the following screen:

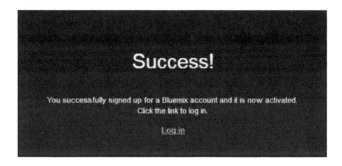

7. Click **Log in** to go to the Bluemix login page. Enter your newly created IBM ID and password to log in:

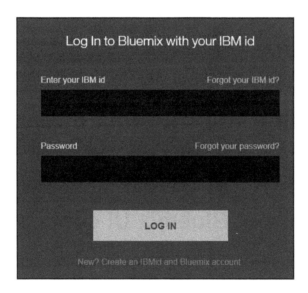

8. On logging in, you will be taken to your dashboard, as shown here:

Congratulations! You have just completed the first step toward getting started with Bluemix.

Understanding the Bluemix dashboard

In this section, let us try to understand some details about the Bluemix Dashboard. This is essential in learning to work with IBM Bluemix.

Key dashboard or Bluemix UI concepts

In this section, we will learn about some of the key concepts used in Bluemix. Your Bluemix account can be administered from the Bluemix console. Understanding of the concepts within Bluemix, which are surfaced on the console, will help you learn how to plan the usage of your account and the resources within it.

Account details

Clicking the icon to the extreme top-right of your dashboard will bring up information on your Bluemix account:

The account details are shown as follows; it displays the account owner's name, registered e-mail address, and organization. You will see your account details here.

Organization

Organization is an all-encompassing entity in the case of a public Bluemix account. This is the topmost level in the hierarchy of entities that a user will work with on Bluemix. For a public Bluemix user who has created a Bluemix account, he is the account owner and organization is his topmost entity. Usually, the account owner's e-mail is defaulted to his organization name. This can be edited by the account owner; we will see how to do that in future sections:

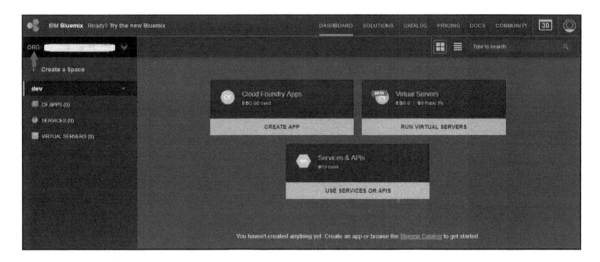

Managing your organization

You can manage your organization by clicking the icon to the extreme top-right corner of the console, also called the **Account Details** view:

This would bring up the following screen, where you can click **Manage Organizations**:

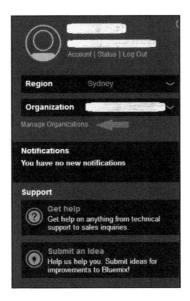

This will bring up the page from where you can administer your Bluemix organization:

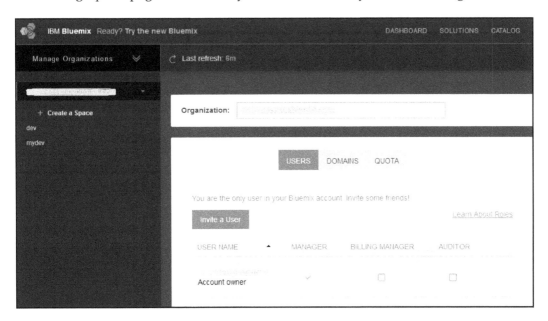

There are three important concepts to be understood here under organization management. You will see that there are three tabs here for **USERS**, **DOMAINS**, and **QUOTA**.

Organization management amounts to actions that you perform with respect to managing the users and domains in the organization.

USERS

The account owner is the default user listed. Now, in a typical development environment, you would want multiple users to be able to access and work on a given space within your organization. This is a must for collaborative development needs. To enable this, you will need to invite a user to your organization and assign him a space.

Click **Invite a User**; you will see the following screen, where you will need to enter the e-mail address of the person you want to invite. You can assign the user you are inviting a role within your organization, which is to manage your organization, or you can simply choose to only give the user access to your space, as a developer:

The user you invite can have an account on Bluemix. You will see his user name listed within your organization once you have invited the user. If you are inviting the user using his e-mail address, which is linked to his IBM ID, then he will be added as a member; if the user does not have an IBM ID, then an IBM ID is created for the user with the e-mail address and he is added as a member. However, in our example, the user already has a Bluemix account linked to the given e-mail address, so he will be added as a collaborator.

Click **INVITE** to invite the user. You will see a confirmation, as follows:

Within your organization, under the **USERS** tab, you will see the new user listed as follows:

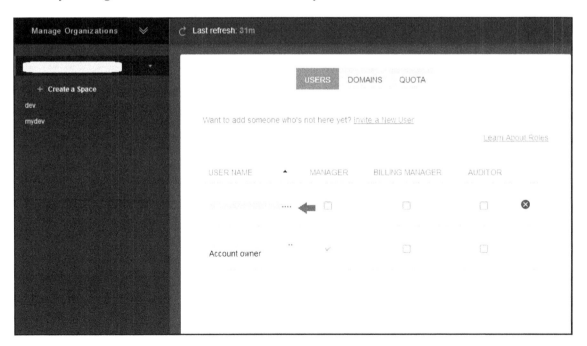

The user that you have invited will be able to see your organization along with his own organization in the account details page; from here he will be able to switch to your organization and will be able to work with the space that you have assigned him to, as shown in the following screenshot:

You can learn more about each of the user roles within an organization and a space by clicking on **Learn About Roles**:

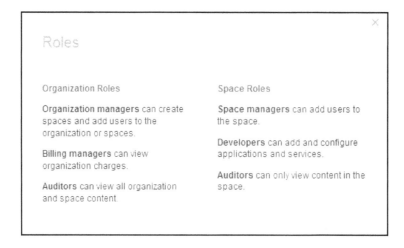

DOMAIN

Click the **DOMAIN** tab from the manage organizations page; you will see the default system domain assigned, which in the case of the demo account would be `au-syd.mybluemix.net`. The public Internet route for your organization is defaulted to the system domain, and the host in the route is usually your application name:

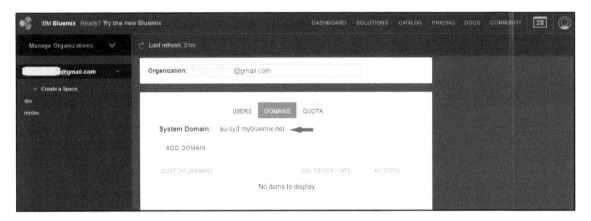

You will be able to add custom domains to your organization by clicking **ADD DOMAIN**. You can associate your applications to use the custom domains instead of the default system domain. The discussion of custom domains is outside the scope of this book. To know more on custom domains, you can refer to the Bluemix documentation at `www.bluemix.net/docs`.

QUOTA

Quota defines the resources allocated to an organization. This will provide information on what is the maximum memory that can be used by applications across spaces in your organization. Quota also provides the total number of cloud service instances that can be created in your organization across spaces. Quota is allocated when the account is created. You can increase your quota by moving to the pay as you go or subscription plans for your Bluemix account. The following screenshot shows the quota for the demo account we are using in this chapter; this would be similar to the quota on the trial account you have created following the steps in this chapter:

Space

Space is a logical grouping of resources on the platform. Multiple Spaces can be created within an organization. Doing so allows the account owner to invite other users to his account and share resources with them by providing resource isolation; he does this by assigning users to a given Space. While inviting users to work on a Space, he can also assign roles for the users that would define what the users can do with the resources and the platform. This is an essential concept, that makes collaborative development a possibility on the platform. In addition, it gives the flexibility of maintaining similar but different environments within the user account. One of the most popular needs to do this would be for someone to isolate test environments from that of development and production. You will notice **dev** is the default Space that is created for your organization:

Creating your own Space

You can create a new Space by clicking **Create a Space** and providing the name of your Space in the dialog that comes up, as shown here:

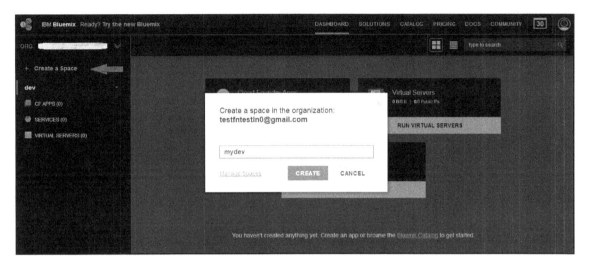

Once your Space is created, you can see it listed to the left, as shown here:

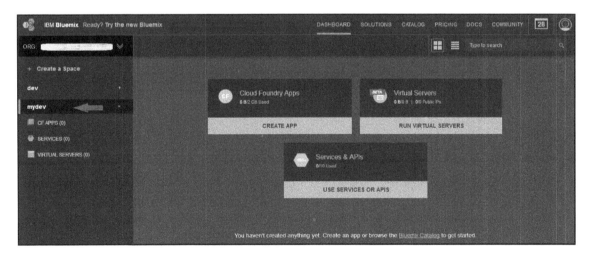

You can work with your Space in the same way as you would with the default **dev** Space. Both the Spaces in your organization have access to and can work with the same set of resources of the platform.

Managing your Space

Go to the account details view and click **Manage Organizations**; you can select the Space you want to manage, as shown here:

In the screenshot, you see that we have selected the **mydev** Space; the user and domain details for this Space can be managed from here. You can remove users in your Space from here. You can also delete the Space from here by clicking on **DELETE**.

Region

Region is an important concept that you need to understand; you see that the Region is displayed in the account details page and this is a drop-down menu, which means that you can switch the region for your account from here:

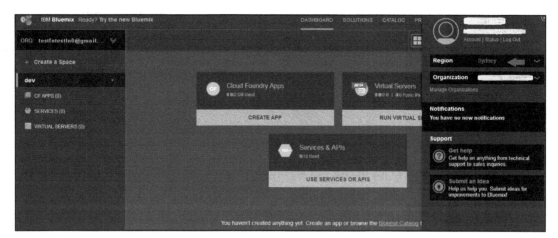

Region-based URLs

The access URLs for directly accessing your account on any of the three data centers are as follows:

- `https://console.ng.bluemix.net` (Dallas, US South)
- `https://console.eu-gb.bluemix.net` (London, UK)
- `https://console.au-syd.bluemix.net` (Sydney, Australia)

Region implies the datacenter where the public Bluemix is hosted. Currently, at the time of writing this book, public Bluemix is available in three datacenters, which can be seen by expanding the drop-down menu on the account details page, explained in the previous section:

The three datacenters are as follows:

- Dallas, US South
- London, United Kingdom
- Sydney, Australia

Any user who creates an account on Bluemix is provided an ORG and default Space in one the datacenters. However, the user can also access his account on any of the other datacenters by creating a Space for his organization.

When you first sign up for your account and go to the login URL from your confirmation e-mail, you will notice being redirected to one of the three URLs mentioned in the preceding information box. That will give you the information on the datacenter where your account and default Space exists.

The demo account used in this chapter is created in the Sydney, Australia datacenter, as you would see from the account details screenshot where Sydney is selected as the default Region. Now, if I would like to use Bluemix from another Region, say, US South for example, I can change the drop-down value of the Region in the account details page to US South. This will automatically redirect me to `https://console.ng.bluemix.net`, which you can witness in the address bar of the browser. Now, since this is a datacenter region that I am going to for the first time since my account creation and since this is not the default datacenter where my default Space was created, you will see the following in your browser:

Working with different Regions

Throughout this book, we will work across Regions on Bluemix and you should now know how to switch your Region using the Bluemix console.

You will see here that you do not have a default Space in this datacenter. You are, however, prompted to create one to continue to use your account on this datacenter.

Enter the name of the Space you would like to create in this region and click **CREATE**:

You will see that my **mydev** Space is created, and now I am on my account on the US South datacenter.

The dashboard for you is displayed as shown in the screenshot. You will observe that the dashboard that you saw when the region of this demo account was Sydney, Australia, is slightly different from the dashboard in the US South region; this is because Bluemix is continuously evolving as a platform. The latest and greatest set of capabilities of the platform are first pushed to the US South datacenter, which is then incrementally and in a phased manner pushed to the other datacenters.

Now let us switch the Region back to Sydney from the account details page.

The number of days your account will be active is indicated on your dashboard, as seen in the following screenshot. Since we have signed up for the free trial period, you will see 30 days indicated in your dashboard. As you progress with Bluemix, with passing days on your account, you will see a countdown to the number of days left for your account:

Clicking the icon showing the number of days left, as shown in the following screenshot, brings up the information on how you can upgrade your Bluemix account from being a trial account to a paid account:

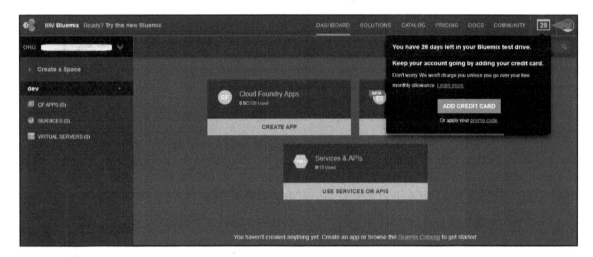

You can get more information on Bluemix pricing by going to `www.bluemix.net/pricing/`.

Summary

In this chapter, we have explored the cloud as-a-service delivery models and have seen how Bluemix fits in the cloud service delivery model. We have also looked at the details of Bluemix as the platform as-a-service offering and the need for it. We learned how to get an account on the public deployment of Bluemix and also looked at the key concepts related to the Bluemix account and account management from the dashboard.

We shall explore the dashboard further in our next chapter. Also in the next chapter, we will learn about the cloud foundry command line utility and how to use it to work with IBM Bluemix. What is more? Get excited to also learn how to build your first Hello World application and deploy it on Bluemix.

2
Building and Deploying Your First Application on IBM Bluemix

After having got an understanding of what is Bluemix from the previous chapter, let us now take the plunge. In this chapter, you will learn a few other important aspects of working with IBM Bluemix. You will be introduced to the Cloud Foundry command-line utility, which is a key component to work your way through the Bluemix platform. You will also learn how to use the command-line utility to deploy a hello world application that you will develop using the example in this chapter. This chapter will further discuss on how you can develop a hello world application using the web IDE on the Bluemix platform and how you can deploy changes to the application in an automated fashion using the DevOps services on Bluemix. Sounds exciting? Yes? Let us get started.

In this chapter, we will be looking at following topics:

- Cloud Foundary command line utility
- Log in to Bluemix using cf cli
- Building your first Hello World application and deploying it on Bluemix
- Updating your application on Bluemix

Cloud Foundry command line utility

Bluemix is a PaaS platform, which is based on open standards. Bluemix at its core is Cloud Foundry, which is an open source community-based project of open standards-based platform as-a-service offering.

 To know more about Cloud Foundry, you can go to `https://www.cloudf oundry.org/learn/features/`.

Cloud Foundry command line utility (**cf cli**) is an interface for the user to interact and work with the Cloud Foundry platform, since Bluemix at its heart is Cloud Foundry, the cf cli can be used to work with the Bluemix platform.

Installing the Cloud Foundry command-line utility

You can step through the following procedure to install the cf cli on your workstation or desktop:

1. Go to `https://github.com/cloudfoundry/cli#downloads` to download the latest version of cf cli installable for your operating system.

   cf cli installable is available for Mac OS X, Linux, and Windows operating systems. For updates on versions and support for operating systems, please make sure to check `https://github.com/cloudfoundry/cli#downloads`.

2. Follow the install instructions provided at `http://docs.cloudfoundry.org/cf-cli/install-go-cli.html`, for your operating system.

For example, installing from the `.pkg` file on your Mac OS X would show the following window on successful installation:

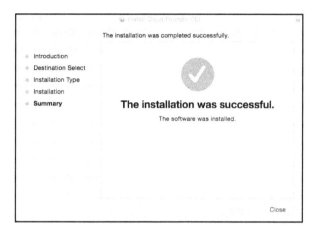

3. Make sure you check your installation by opening the command prompt (if Windows) or the terminal window (if Mac OS X) and typing the following command:

```
cf
```

4. If installed successfully, you will see the help contents displayed, as shown here, for example, when the command is run on a terminal window of Mac OS X:

```
Last login: Mon Apr 18 12:19:04 on console
xXXXX-MacBook-Pro:~ xxxxx$ cf
NAME:
  cf - A command line tool to interact with Cloud Foundry
USAGE:
  cf [global options] command [arguments...] [command options]
VERSION:
  6.17.0+5d0be0a-2016-04-15
GETTING STARTED:
  help                            Show help
  version                         Print the version
  login                           Log user in
  logout                          Log user out
  passwd                          Change user password
  target                          Set or view the targeted org
                                  or space
............
............
xXXXX-MacBook-Pro:~ xXXXX$
```

Log in to Bluemix using cf cli

After having installed cf cli, let us now learn how to log in to your Bluemix account using the cf cli. In this chapter, we will use a terminal window to explain how to use cf cli; the cf commands and steps explained are similar even if you were to use cf cli on Windows command prompt or Linux terminal.

Log in to your Bluemix account

Follow the steps given to log in to your Bluemix account:

1. Open the terminal window and enter the following command:

   `cf login`

2. On hitting *Enter*, you will see that you will be prompted to enter an API endpoint; this is required if you want to log in to a specific region. The API endpoints are based on the regions where public Bluemix is available:

   - The API endpoint for Dallas, US region is
     `https://api.ng.bluemix.net`
   - The API endpoint for London, UK region is
     `https://api.eu-gb.bluemix.net`
   - The API endpoint for Sydney, Australia region is
     `https://api.au-syd.bluemix.net`

   Since the account you have created in Chapter 1, *Saying Hello to IBM Bluemix*, is in the Sydney, Australia region, we will provide the API endpoint as `https://api.au-syd.bluemix.net`:

3. Next, you will be prompted to enter your e-mail address, which is also your log in username, and your password. Once you provide these and hit *Enter*, your authentication details will be validated. Once authenticated, you will see that you will be logged in to your default target organization. You will then be provided with options on the Space you would like to work with, within your Bluemix organization:

4. Select the Space you want to work with by keying in 1 or 2 (from the options shown). Hit *Enter* and you will be successfully logged in to your space within your organization on Bluemix where you can deploy your applications or work with service instances or your applications. This completes your login to your Bluemix account from cf cli, as shown in the following screenshot:

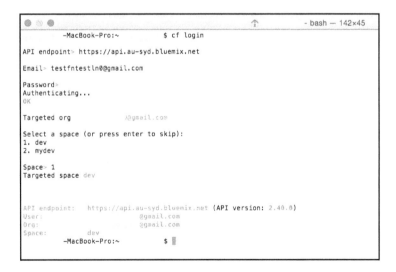

You can log in to any region where you have Space created for your organization, by using the API endpoint. It can so happen that using `cf login` may default to the API endpoint you have used earlier. To override this option, you can use the following command to log in:

```
cf login -a https://api.ng.bluemix.net
```

The following screenshot shows the output of the preceding command:

Here you see that since there is only one space in the organization for the user in the US region, the login command defaults the user to that Space, **mydev**.

There are a whole lot of operations you can do with cf cli, however we will learn more about using cf cli in our subsequent sections, where we will look at building a hello world application and deploying it on Bluemix.

Building your first Hello World application and deploying it on Bluemix

In our first Hello World example we shall look at how easy it is to get started with a Hello World application using Bluemix. For this we will use the Bluemix dashboard to work with the platform. In the subsequent section we will look at using the same Hello World application and we will learn to use cf cli to deploy the application on Bluemix.

Understanding some more Bluemix concepts

Before you start creating the Hello World application, there are a few aspects of the Bluemix dashboard that need understanding. Log in to your Bluemix account by going to `https://c onsole.au-syd.bluemix.net`. You will be taken to the dashboard, as shown in the following screenshot:

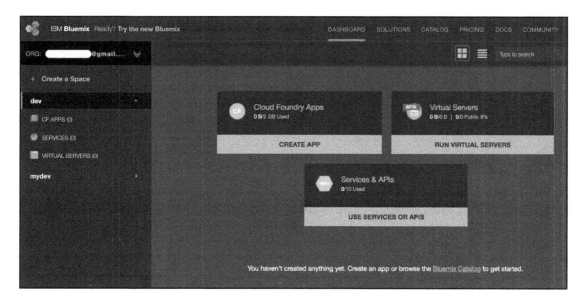

You will see that from your dashboard you can work with applications and services. Applications are deployable code that can be run on a compute environment on the Bluemix platform. Applications are what you build and deploy.

Services are IBM, third-party or community software that is provided on the Bluemix platform. Users can create service instances and can bind them to the applications they develop and deploy on Bluemix. By doing this, their applications can leverage the functionality of the software offered as services on the Bluemix platform. An example of a service would be a database, which is a bare bones requirement for any modern or legacy applications, that deal with data.

 Virtual Servers or VMs, Containers, and OpenWhisk are compute environments that provide options for users where they can deploy their applications. Cloud Foundry is the default compute environment for the Bluemix platform. At the time of writing this book the Sydney region does not have support for Containers and OpenWhisk.

The following screenshot shows the compute environments that we discussed, available in the US region:

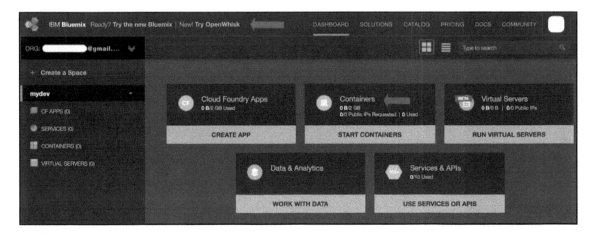

Runtimes is the execution environment for your application code. For example, if you are developing a Java Spring-based web application then the execution environment for your application would require a web server or an application server that can run Java code additionally you would also need the execution environment to have the necessary libraries for the Spring framework, so that your application code can execute. This is typically what a runtime would be.

The runtime options available can be seen by clicking on **CATALOG** option on the Bluemix dashboard. At the time of writing this book the runtimes available are as shown in the following screenshot:

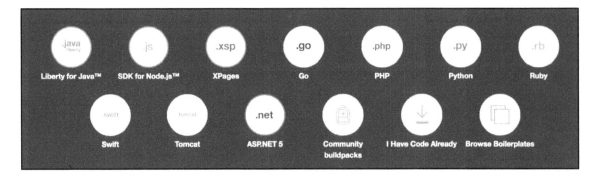

Buildpacks are a mechanism to define runtime environment along with dependencies to Cloud Foundry. Specifying a buildpack when deploying your application will make sure that Cloud Foundry can get the necessary dependencies to build your execution environment. Buildpack is an important mechanism of bringing in support for programming languages and frameworks that are not claimed to be supported out of the box on the Bluemix platform. We will learn more about it, later in this book. Community Buildpacks, shown in the following screenshot, explains how and where to get the Cloud Foundry-compatible buildpacks, so that you can deploy applications written in programming languages or frameworks that are not supported out of the box on the Bluemix platform:

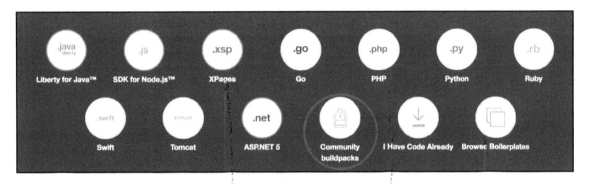

The steps to deploy an application using **Community buildpacks** would be as follows:

1. Look up for a Cloud Foundry-compatible buildpack for your programming language or framework from `https://github.com/cloudfoundry-community/cf-docs-contrib/wiki/Buildpacks`.
2. Copy the GitHub URL for the buildpack you want to use.
3. Use cf cli to log in to your Bluemix account, organization, and Space, where you would want to deploy your application.
4. Execute the following `cf` command:

```
cf push {$APP_NAME} -b {$GIT_REPO_URL}
```

An example command would be :

```
cf push timeticker -b https://github.com/spiegela/cf-buildpack-erlang
```

Bluemix is an evolving platform and it is important to note that the screenshots may look different with the updates to Bluemix platform. The preceding screenshots on the runtimes supported are from the classic view of Bluemix console. At the time of writing this book, we have a newer version of the console that is available, which can be used by switching to it. Click the **Try the new Bluemix** link, to work with the newer Bluemix console:

The runtimes for Cloud Foundry-based applications on Bluemix, as shown in the following screenshot, is the newer version of the console:

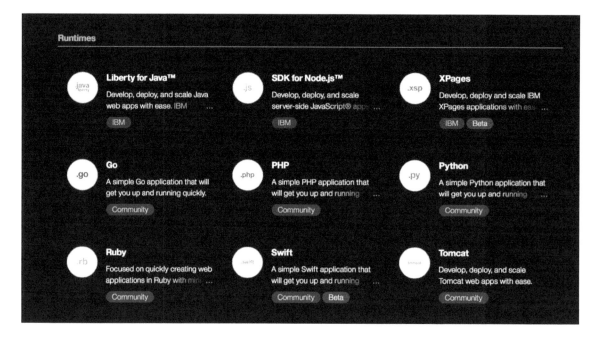

 In the rest of our chapters in this book, we will be using screenshots from Bluemix newer console as well as the classic console. We will be providing the information on if the screenshot if from newer or classic console. You can use one of the options to work with your Bluemix console.

Boilerplates are application development patterns, which have been standardized across categories and have been provided as templates for Bluemix user. The use of these boilerplates to create an application expedites the application development by seamlessly creating the necessary service instances and application stub with execution environment. Let us understand this further by looking at one of the boilerplate example from the list of supported boilerplate templates available on Bluemix, which is shown in the following screenshot. This screenshot is from the newer Bluemix console:

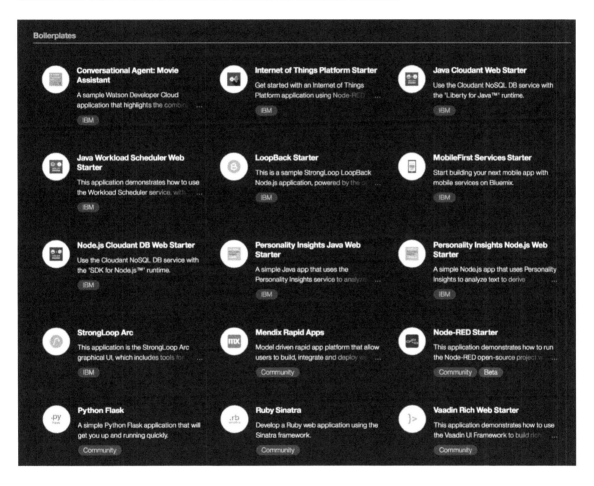

Clicking one of the preceding boilerplates, say the **Java Cloud Web Starter** boilerplate, would bring up the details related to this boilerplate as shown in the following screenshot:

Here you will notice that the boilerplate consists of a runtime for Java applications, which is the IBM Liberty for Java application server; the boilerplate also contains the Cloudant NoSQL DB as a service. Pricing plans are shown separately for the runtime and for the Cloudant service, which you can see by selecting the Cloudant NoSQL DB service. When a user selects this boilerplate to create an application, then the platform creates an execution environment for his web application by provisioning Liberty for Java. Additionally, a service instance of Cloudant NoSQL DB is created in the user space, an application stub in Java is created and deployed in Liberty runtime. The application stub will have minimalistic functions that involves talking to the Cloudant NoSQL DB service instance as well. What this provides is a great starting point for the user to build web applications that uses an application server and a database.

Similarly, you see that there are other boilerplates that allow you to get started with creating applications using different programming languages, frameworks, or services. We will be creating our first Hello World application using one of the boilerplates, and during this exercise you will learn the process of using boilerplates, editing application stub, and deploying and re-deploying application on Bluemix.

Creating your Hello World application on Bluemix using a boilerplate

You can follow the steps given here to start creating your first application on Bluemix. We will use the boilerplate as our getting started mechanism. We will be using the newer Bluemix console for most of our screenshots in this section:

1. Log in to the Bluemix console or dashboard, use your IBM ID to log in, as was explained in Chapter 1, *Saying Hello to IBM Bluemix*.

    At the time of writing this book, the URL to directly go to the new Bluemix console in Sydney region is https://new-console.au-syd.bluemix.net/.

2. You will be taken to a landing page, as shown in the following screenshot:

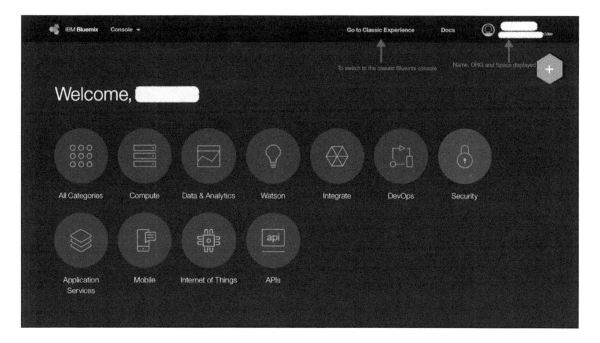

3. Click **Compute**, to be taken to the compute options available in your region. Since at the time of writing this book the only compute option available in the Sydney region is **CF Applications**, which is the Cloud Foundry-based compute environment for your applications. If we go to other regions, such as US and UK, you will see additional compute options such as Containers, OpenWhisk, and Virtual Servers. To build this application let us switch region to Dallas, US, as explained in Chapter 1, *Saying Hello to IBM Bluemix*, and then let us go to **CF Applications** under **Compute**:

4. Click the icon next to **Get started now**, as shown in the preceding screenshot. You will be taken to the page which displays all the supported runtimes and available boilerplates:

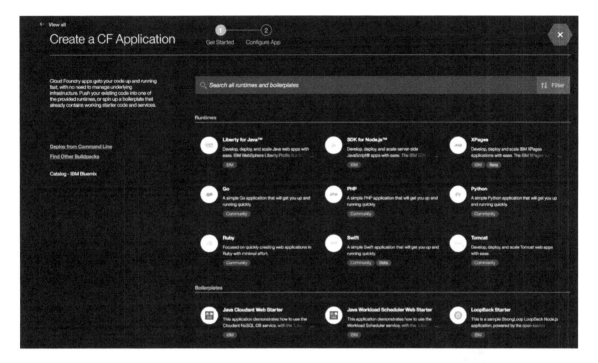

5. You can choose to start your application creation by choosing a runtime or by choosing a boilerplate. In this section we will look at creating the application by choosing a boilerplate. We will use the **Personality Insights Java Web Starter** boilerplate:

6. You will be taken to the page which gives you more information on the boilerplate, such as the runtime and services that make up the boilerplate, as well as pricing metrics for them.

During the running of this example, if your free trial account is valid, you do not have to concern yourself with the pricing yet, you will be within the free tier usage for the runtime and service. If you would like to use the application or service beyond the free trial period, then refer to the procedure of converting your trial Bluemix account to a paid account and gain access to services with powerful and feature rich services along with continued use of resources to keep your application live. You can refer to www.bluemix.net/pricing.

7. As shown in the following screenshot, you will need to provide a unique name to your application in the **App name:** field, the **Host name:** field usually defaults to the **App name:** field. You can leave the rest of fields with their default values. Plans for runtime or service defines their respective charging metrics:

8. This is how a filled out screen would look, for example:

9. Click **Create** at the bottom, this will create the service instance of **Personality Insights**, an execution environment with IBM Liberty for Java application server, and an application stub in Java, that works with the **Personality Insights** service instance:

10. The **Create** operation would take few seconds before it completes. Once this operation completes, you will see the following screenshot. You can see the status of your application stub, as highlighted:

11. You can see in the preceding screenshot that you have three options on how you can work with your application stub. You are also provided inline instructions on how you can get started with each of the following options:

    - Eclipse Tools for Bluemix
    - Command-line interface
    - Git

12. You can also see tabs to work with your deployed application, you can look at application logs, monitor your application, look at the application's use of the runtime capacity, and so on, through the respective tabs provided in the preceding screenshot, such as:

- **Overview**: It gives a snapshot view of the application stats such as number of instances, memory usage, activity logs and so on, as shown in the following screenshot, which is for the application we created:

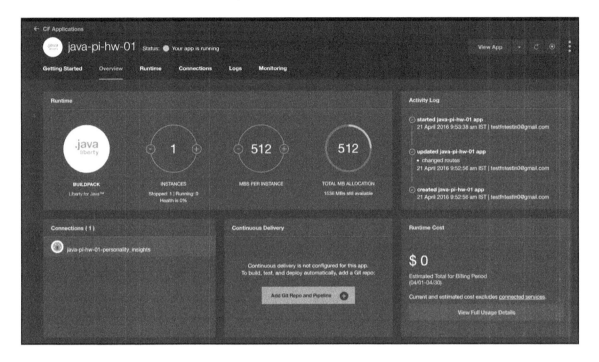

- **Runtime**: It gives the information on the usage of the runtime capacity, in our case, the memory allocated and used by the Java application as the runtime charge metrics is the memory used by the application, measured in GB Hour. This is shown in the **Memory and Instances** tab; this information is similar to what we see under **Runtime** in the preceding **Overview** screenshot. The **Runtime** tab also has two additional tabs, **Environment Variables** and **Files**. **Environment Variables** shows the information on variables used by the application to connect to external services, as shown in the following screenshot:

- **Files**: This tab shows the files relevant to buildpack (Liberty for Java in this case), application-related files, log files related to application staging and deployment on Bluemix, and so on, as shown in the following screenshot:

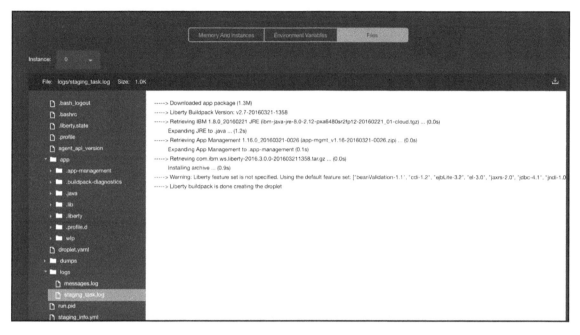

- **Connections**: It gives information on the services used by the application and the credentials and associated information to connect to the service instance:

- **Logs**: It gives the handle to logs that can be filtered based on the component it belongs to. The following screenshot shows the logs for the application, based on selection from the drop-down shown:

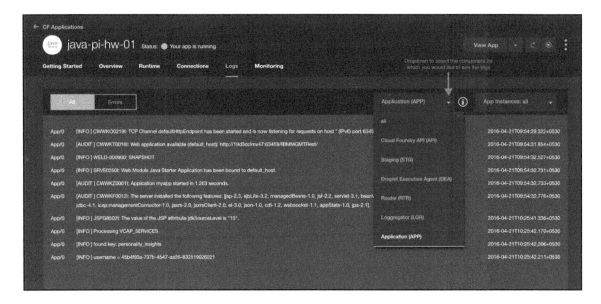

- **Monitoring**: It provides a visualization of the application availability stats, as shown, for the application created, in the following screenshot:

Since your application status is **Running**, you will be able to launch your application by clicking on **View App**, as shown in the following screenshot:

This will take you to the application URL or Route, which is a public URL for your application, accessible over the Internet. In case of the application you have created, you will be taken to its route, which is `http://java-pi-hw-1.mybluemix.net`. The application brings up a UI that talks about the **Personality Insights** service and has a text box that allows your application user to enter any text, which can be analyzed for personality traits, leveraging the cognitive service of **Personality Insights** that you have used in your application. There is default text that prepopulates this text box. When you launch your application URL, when you hit on **Analyze** for this text, you will see the results of the personality traits derived from this text, as shown in the following screenshots:

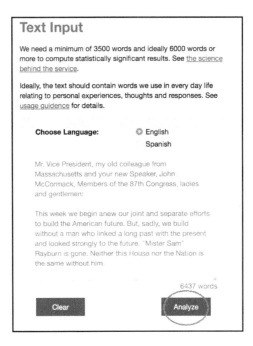

Personality traits after analyzing the default text is shown as follows:

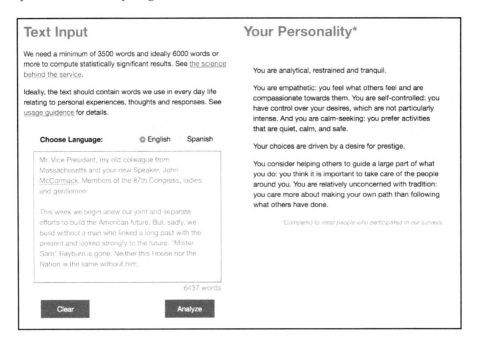

Details on the analysis and visualization is provided as a result, as well:

Data Behind Your Personality

Name	Value ± Sampling Error
Big 5	
Openness	**95% (± 5%)**
Adventurousness	88% (± 4%)
Artistic interests	62% (± 9%)
Emotionality	22% (± 4%)
Imagination	89% (± 5%)
Intellect	96% (± 4%)
Authority-challenging	88% (± 7%)
Conscientiousness	**76% (± 6%)**
Achievement striving	74% (± 8%)
Cautiousness	91% (± 8%)
Dutifulness	47% (± 5%)
Orderliness	21% (± 6%)
Self-discipline	43% (± 4%)
Self-efficacy	93% (± 8%)
Extraversion	**23% (± 4%)**
Activity level	39% (± 6%)
Assertiveness	21% (± 7%)
Cheerfulness	14% (± 9%)
Excitement-seeking	2% (± 7%)
Outgoing	55% (± 6%)

Visualization of Personality Data

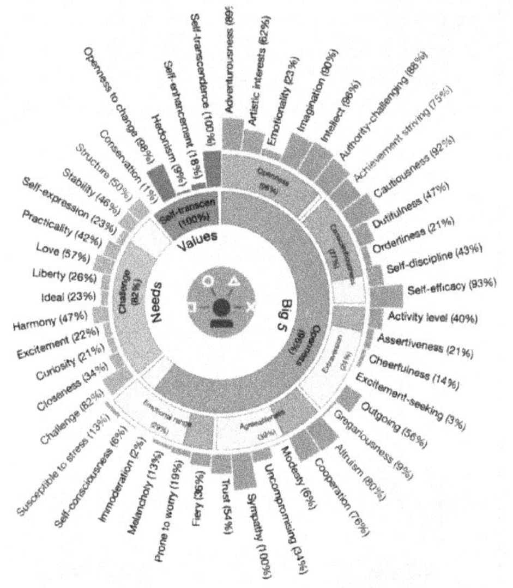

This application can be used to cognitively understand unstructured text and analyze it to look for personality traits to arrive at a view of personality data as derived from unstructured data related to a given personality. For example, you can search for Wikipedia text on any known personality, for example, in the following screenshots, we have demonstrated the personality traits of Swami Vivekananda as derived by using your application. The data on Swami Vivekananda we have input in the application is sourced from Wikipedia.

The results are as shown in the following screenshot:

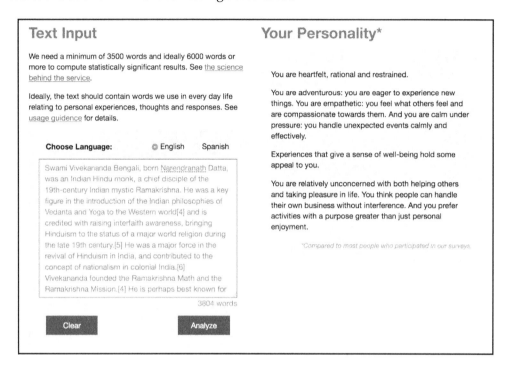

 The accuracy of the results is higher depending on the volume of data input and the quality of data.

Further analytics on the personality data is as shown in the following screenshot:

Data Behind Your Personality		Visualization of Personality Data

Name	Value ± Sampling Error
Big 5	
Openness	**98% (± 5%)**
Adventurousness	100% (± 4%)
Artistic interests	69% (± 9%)
Emotionality	2% (± 4%)
Imagination	95% (± 5%)
Intellect	98% (± 5%)
Authority-challenging	94% (± 7%)
Conscientiousness	**94% (± 6%)**
Achievement striving	87% (± 8%)
Cautiousness	97% (± 8%)
Dutifulness	18% (± 5%)
Orderliness	1% (± 6%)
Self-discipline	84% (± 4%)
Self-efficacy	90% (± 8%)
Extraversion	**10% (± 4%)**
Activity level	41% (± 6%)
Assertiveness	6% (± 7%)
Cheerfulness	3% (± 9%)
Excitement-seeking	0% (± 7%)

You have successfully created your first application on Bluemix. Next, we will see how you can work with the source files to make changes to your first application. Though this application is more than just a Hello World application, we can call it a Hello World as this is as good as your starting point on creating and deploying applications on Bluemix.

Updating your application on Bluemix

In this section, we will look at two aspects of application update, one is the update to the application source, and the other is the update to the application deployment on Bluemix.

Downloading the source files for your starter or Hello World application

Follow these steps given to download the source files for your application:

1. Go to the **Getting Started** tab, as shown in the following screenshot; here, select the option of using the command-line interface:

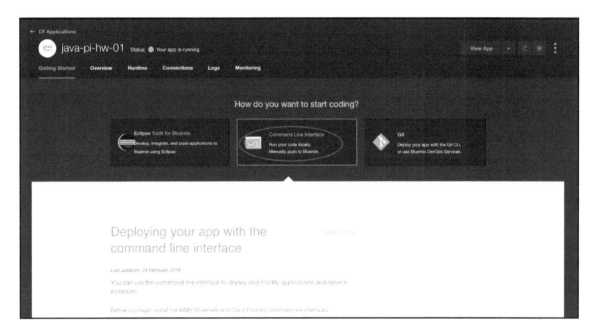

2. On this page, you will find the steps to get started with your application code using the command line interface. Since we have already downloaded the cf cli, we will only be downloading the application code now. Click the **DOWNLOAD STARTER CODE** button, to download the source files for your application:

3. Move the downloaded files to a folder on your local machine, for example, projects:

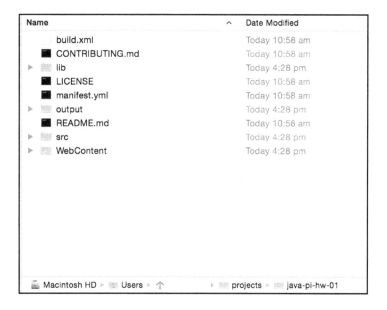

It is important to understand the `manifest.yml` file. This is the file where you can specify parameters to instruct cloud foundry at application deployment time. You can define the number of instances, memory for your application, services used, and so on, within the `manifest.yml` file. To know more about the manifest file, refer to `https://docs.cloudfoundry.org/devguide/deploy-apps/manifest.html`.

4. You can open the `manifest.yml` file, to see the deployable artifact for your application. This is how the manifest file for your application looks:

```
applications:
- path: output/webApp.war
  memory: 512M
  instances: 1
  domain: mybluemix.net
  name: java-pi-hw-01
  host: java-pi-hw-01
  disk_quota: 1024M
  services:
  - java-pi-hw-01-personality_insights
```

5. From the manifest file, you will notice that the deployable artifact for your application is the `webApp.war` file.

6. You can choose to make any change locally on the application file. For this example, we choose to change the default text input that appears on your application screen. We will do this by modifying the `en.txt` file, inside the `WebContent/text` folder. We shall edit the contents on this text file to show text from Wikipedia on any other famous personality, for example, Adolf Hitler. Once we edit and save locally the `en.txt` file, we need to locally build the application files, for which we will use ant:

```
●  ●  ●                                                  🔲 java-pi-hw-01 — bash — 142×45
           .-MacBook-Pro:java-pi-hw-01 sreelathas$ pwd
/Users/           /projects/java-pi-hw-01
           .-MacBook-Pro:java-pi-hw-01 sreelathas$ ls
CONTRIBUTING.md README.md     build          lib            output
LICENSE         WebContent    build.xml      manifest.yml   src
Sreelathas-MacBook-Pro:java-pi-hw-01          .$ ant
Buildfile: /Users/          ./projects/java-pi-hw-01/build.xml

clean:
    [delete] Deleting directory /Users/            /projects/java-pi-hw-01/build
    [delete] Deleting: /Users/              /projects/java-pi-hw-01/output/webApp.war

init:
    [mkdir] Created dir: /Users/            /projects/java-pi-hw-01/build
    [mkdir] Created dir: /Users/'           /projects/java-pi-hw-01/build/bin

build-project:
    [echo] WebApp: /Users/            /projects/java-pi-hw-01/build.xml
    [javac] Compiling 1 source file to /Users/          ;/projects/java-pi-hw-01/build/bin
    [javac] warning: [options] bootstrap class path not set in conjunction with -source 1.6
    [javac] 1 warning

build-war:
    [war] Building war: /Users/            /projects/java-pi-hw-01/output/webApp.war

build:

BUILD SUCCESSFUL
Total time: 1 second
           .-MacBook-Pro:java-pi-hw-01             $ ▊
```

 Instructions on installing ant on your local machine is beyond the scope of discussion here. You can refer to instructions here `http://ant.apache.or g/manual/install.html` or to similar sites for information on installing ant on your local machine.

7. Open a terminal window and change the directory to your project or application root folder, and log in to Bluemix using cf cli, as explained earlier. Now execute the following command to push your application changes or updates to Bluemix:

```
cf push java-pi-hw-01
```

8. The results of execution of the command will be as shown in the following screenshot:

```
$ ......._s-MacBook-Pro:java-pi-hw-01 $ ..... _s$ cf login -a https://api.ng.bluemix.net
API endpoint: https://api.ng.bluemix.net

Email> t._'''''s0@gmail.com
Password>
Authenticating...
OK

Targeted org .........@gmail.com

Targeted space mydev


API endpoint:   https://api.ng.bluemix.net (API version: 2.44.0)
User:           .........@gmail.com
Org:            .........@gmail.com
Space:          mydev
$ ......._s-MacBook-Pro:java-pi-hw-01 $ ......s$ pwd
/Users/s........./projects/java-pi-hw-01
   .....s-MacBook-Pro:java-pi-hw-01 $ ......s$ cf push java-pi-hw-01
Using manifest file ................./java-pi-hw-01/manifest.yml

Updating app java-pi-hw-01 in org .........@gmail.com / space mydev as .........@gmail.com...
OK

Using route java-pi-hw-01.mybluemix.net
Uploading java-pi-hw-01...
Uploading app files from: /var/folders/81/g_8p5x257c3bjjsbmfnymyf00000gq/T/unzipped-app990900661
Uploading 428.7K, 55 files
Done uploading
OK
Binding service java-pi-hw-01-cloudantNoSQLDB-.......... to app java-pi-hw-01 in org .........@gmail.com / space mydev as .........@gmail.com...
OK

Stopping app java-pi-hw-01 in org .........@gmail.com / space mydev as .........@gmail.com...
OK

Starting app java-pi-hw-01 in org .........@gmail.com / space mydev as .........@gmail.com...
-----> Downloaded app package (1.3M)
-----> Downloaded app buildpack cache (4.0K)
-----> Liberty Buildpack Version: v2.7-20160321-1358
-----> Retrieving IBM 1.8.0_20160221 JRE (ibm-java-jre-8.0-2.12-pxa6480sr2fp12-20160221_01-cloud.tgz) ... (0.0s)
       Expanding JRE to .java ... (1.5s)
-----> Retrieving App Management 1.16.0_20160321-0026 (app-mgmt_v1.16-20160321-0026.zip) ... (0.0s)
       Expanding App Management to .app-management (0.1s)
-----> Retrieving com.ibm.ws.liberty-2016.3.0.0-201603211358.tar.gz ... (0.0s)
       Installing archive ... (1.2s)
-----> Warning: Liberty feature set is not specified. Using the default feature set: ["beanValidation-1.1", "cdi-1.2", "ejbLite-3.2", "el-3.0", "jaxrs-2.0", "jdbc-4.1", "jndi-1.0", "jpa-2.1", "jsf-2.2", "jsonp-1.0", "jsp-2.3", "managedBea
ns-1.0", "servlet-3.1", "websocket-1.1"]. For the best results, explicitly set the features via the JBP_CONFIG_LIBERTY environment variable or deploy the application as a server directory or packaged server with a custom server.xml file.
-----> Liberty buildpack is done creating the droplet
-----> Uploading droplet (120M)

0 of 1 instances running, 1 starting
0 of 1 instances running, 1 starting
0 of 1 instances running, 1 starting
0 of 1 instances running, 1 starting
1 of 1 instances running

App started

OK

App java-pi-hw-01 was started using this command `.liberty/initial_startup.rb`

Showing health and status for app java-pi-hw-01 in org .........@gmail.com / space mydev as .........@gmail.com...
OK

requested state: started
instances: 1/1
usage: 512M x 1 instances
urls: java-pi-hw-01.mybluemix.net
```

9. Once your application update is completed, you can go to the application route or URL, to check if your update is reflected. In the following screenshot, you will see that the default **Text Input** is now changed to the text that we updated in the `en.txt` file, from the application files:

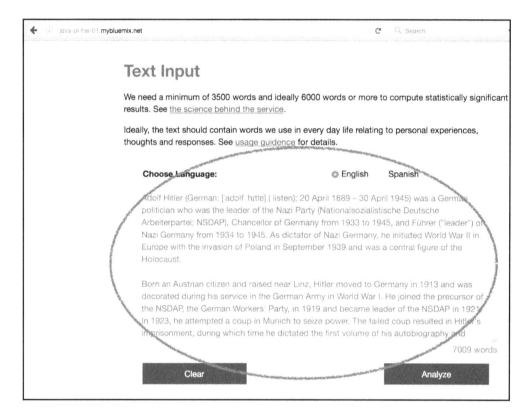

Summary

In this chapter, we learned about installing and using the Cloud Foundry command-line utility to work with Bluemix. Further, we learned about various concepts, such as services, runtimes, boilerplates, and so on, related to the Bluemix platform. We took the first step in application development and deployment by creating a starter or a Hello World application using boilerplate on Bluemix. In this chapter, you also learned how to get the starter code for your Hello World application and how to make changes to it locally, and how to push the updated application to Bluemix; we used cf cli to demonstrate this. In the next chapter, you will learn more ways and techniques to work with Bluemix and your applications. We will see how by learning how to extend existing applications.

3

Extending an Application and Configuring for Continuous Delivery Using DevOps Services

Ready to dive a little deeper into understanding the Bluemix platform? Yes? Great! Let us get started by looking at what you will get to learn in this chapter. In this chapter, you will learn how to compose an extensible application by using services from the Bluemix catalog; we will take you through this using a sample application. We will also learn what continuous delivery is and how would you should be configuring your application to achieve continuous delivery using the DevOps services provided on the Bluemix platform. You will also learn how to extend this application easily to incorporate more functional capabilities.

In this chapter, we will be covering the following topics:

- DevOps services and the delivery pipeline
- Configuring the delivery pipeline for your application
- Configuring continuous delivery for your application
- Extending the application

DevOps services and the delivery pipeline

The delivery pipeline is the mechanism for configuring continuous delivery in the agile application development and deployment lifecycle. The delivery pipeline is a service in the DevOps category. A suite of other services are also available under the DevOps category on Bluemix. The services available in this category at the time of writing this book is as shown in the following screenshot:

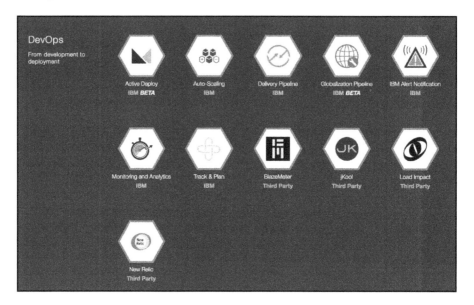

Configuring the delivery pipeline for your application

Before we look at how to configure the delivery pipeline, we will need to create an application that we will use for illustration. So let us get started by creating a starter application by using a boilerplate, as we did in the previous chapter. This time, we will use the Internet of Things boilerplate to create the starter application. We have chosen this boilerplate for few reasons, as follows:

- Understanding how to write applications that are wired and not coded
- Getting a feel for writing or wiring applications in Node-RED
- Using IBM's Internet of Things capabilities, which can be used to create applications that work with device data.

Creating the sample application

Having finished `Chapter 2`, *Building and Deploying Your First Application on IBM Bluemix*, you will be now well-versed in creating an application using boilerplate; hence, we will not be going through all the steps of application creation in detail in this section.

URLs for accessing the new Bluemix console are as follows:

Datacenter	URL
United States	`https://console.ng.bluemix.net/`
United Kingdom	`https://console.eu-gb.bluemix.net/`
Sydney	`https://console.au-syd.bluemix.net/`

Follow these steps to create the sample application; the sample application will be an Internet of Things example application:

1. Log in to your Bluemix account and choose the Space where you want to create your application:

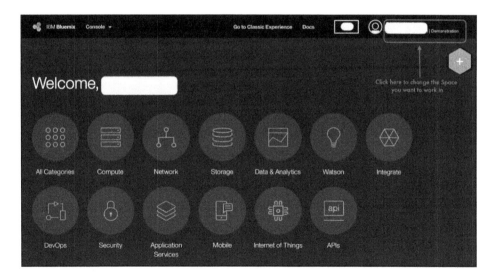

2. Make sure the region you are in is either US South or United Kingdom. Switch the region if you are in the Sydney region.
3. Click **Compute**.
4. Choose **Cloud Foundry Applications**.

5. Click the + icon above **Get Started Now**:

6. In the **Search** field, type `Internet of Things`.
7. Click the boilerplate displaying Internet of Things Platform Starter:

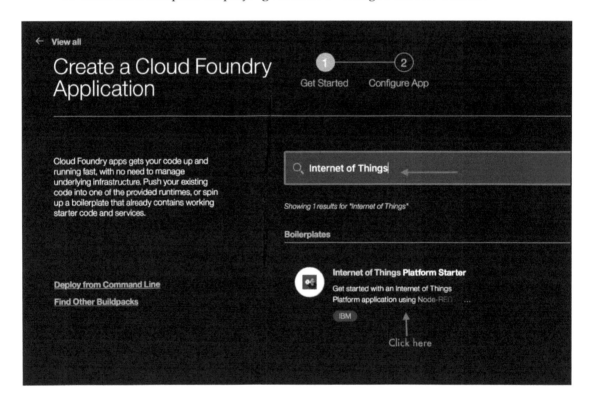

8. Fill out the fields as shown in the following screenshot. Make sure your **App name** is unique if your **Host name** is defaulted to the **App name** field:

9. You will see that SDK for Node.js is the runtime created, and Cloudant NoSQL DB is the database service that will be added to your Space once you click **CREATE**.

Your application is created and started along with the services in the boilerplate-Cloudant NoSQL DB, in this case:

Learning to wire applications using Node-RED

Before we look at the application we just deployed, let us understand what Node-RED is and how to compose applications using the Node-RED editor.

Node-RED is a community-based tool that is used to wire APIs, services, or devices in ways that create innovative applications. Applications developed with Node-RED run on Node.js runtime.

 Find out more about Node-RED by going to `http://nodered.org`.

Node-RED provides a browser-based editor to compose or wire applications. The components that can be wired together are displayed in the editor palette and are called nodes. The list of nodes available in the palette is extensible; you can write your own nodes, add them to your Node-RED package, and even contribute them to the community.

 To find out more about how to extend your Node-RED palette, you can refer to `http://nodered.org/docs/creating-nodes/`.

With this introduction to Node-RED, let us start from where we left off in our previous section:

1. Click the route that is created for your application, which is `http://bm-learning -3-1.eu-gb.mybluemix.net`, in the case of the following screenshot:

2. On the page that is displayed after clicking the application route, click **Go to your Node-RED flow editor**:

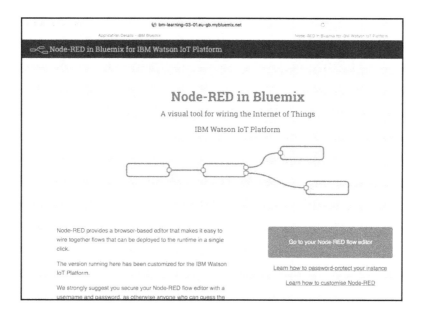

This welcome page can be modified to suit your application, if you desire.

3. Click **Go to your Node-RED flow editor** to open the Node-RED editor:

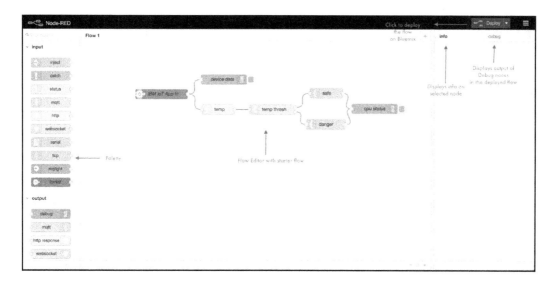

To compose applications, you simply need to drag and drop the nodes from the palette to the flow editor and wire them.

4. Double-click on each node to configure it.
5. Click **Deploy** to deploy your application on Bluemix.

Since we have used the Internet of Things boilerplate to reach the Node-RED editor, you will see that a starter application has already been created by Bluemix.

This starter application reads device data using the IBM Internet of Things node. The device data is expected to push temperature readings to the flow. This is then checked for its value, and if the value is below a certain reference value, the output indicates safe limits. If the temperature is above the reference range, the output indicates it as critical. In the starter application, the output is pushed to the debug node, which can be seen in the debug window. Let us first understand this flow in detail by looking at each node and its configuration:

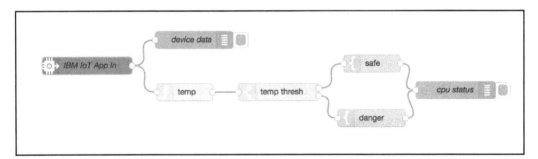

The ibmiot node

The ibmiot node is an input node that receives data from devices using IBM Internet of Things Foundation. The detailed information on this node can be seen in the **info** tab after selecting the node in the flow editor.

Configuring the ibmiot node

Double-click on the node to open its configuration window, which is as shown in the following screenshot:

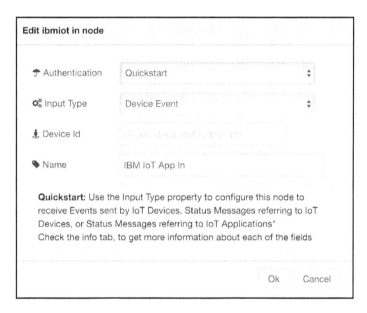

You will see that you can specify the **Authentication** mechanism to connect to your device, define the **Input type** for the trigger or data that you want to listen to, configure the **Device Id** of the device you want to receive data from, and the node **Name** field, where you can specify the name of your **ibmiot** node in the flow.

In this starter application example, we will be using a mock device for which we will be using the quickstart facility of the IBM Internet of Things Foundation. Hence, you will see that the **Authentication** field is left with the value of `Quickstart`, **Input Type** with the value of `Device Event`, and **Name** with the value of `IBM Iot App In`. To configure the **Device Id** field, go to `https://quickstart.internetofthings.ibmcloud.com/iotsensor/` to get a mock device.

You will be provided with a simulated sensor device that outputs temperature, humidity, and object temperature:

 Do not close the browser where you have the simulated device running; closing the browser would lose the device corresponding to the device ID you got earlier.

The identifier on the top right-hand corner, as shown in the following screenshot, is the device identifier for this simulated device. This is the identifier that you will need to input to the Device Id field in the ibmiot configuration dialog box:

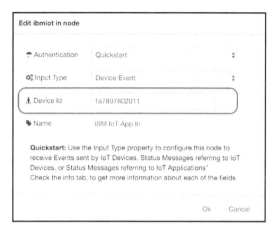

Click **Ok**. This will enable the **Deploy** button. Click **Deploy** to deploy the change to Bluemix:

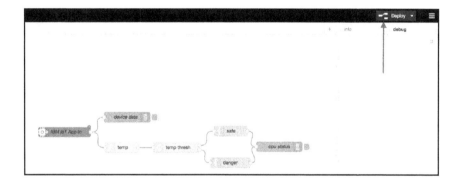

The debug node

The output of any node is displayed on the debug tab of the sidebar of the flow editor by using the **debug** node in the flow, as shown. In this starter application flow, two debug nodes are wired, named device data and cpu status. The device data debug node outputs the device data received by the **ibmiot** node. The **cpu status** debug node outputs the final results as a result of execution of the logic written within the function nodes and formats specified within the template nodes.

The following screenshot shows the output from the two debug nodes in the flow, in the debug editor, after the **Device Id** field is configured in the **ibmiot** node:

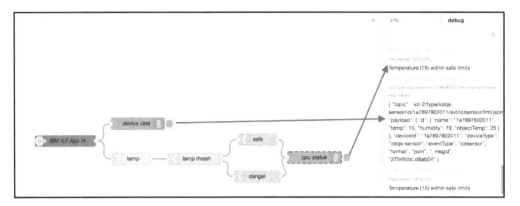

The function node

You can use the function node to write code to manipulate the message passed as a JavaScript Object. For this starter application, the function node carries the code, as shown in the following screenshot. The temperature is extracted from the message payload and passed on to the next node:

For more information about working with the function node, you can refer to `http://nodered.org/docs/writing-functions.html`.

The switch node

This node is used to route messages based on the value of the property in the message object. Routes are defined by defining rules on the switch node. The number of rules defined creates an equal number of output endpoints on the node, which can be wired to define individual flows paths. In this starter application, the switch node is used to check the temperature value from the input message object and define rules based on the temperature threshold value of 40 degrees:

The template node

This node is used to display the property based on the template provided. In the starter application flow, we see there are two template nodes, **safe** and **danger**. Both of these nodes display the temperature property based on the template definition; the following screenshot shows the configuration for the **safe** node:

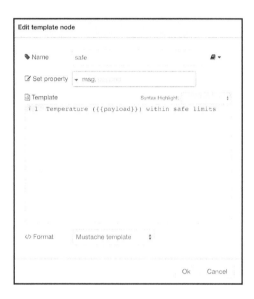

The following screenshot shows the configuration for the **danger** node:

Configuring continuous delivery for your application

Let us see how we can configure the delivery pipeline for the application we just created, so that any changes to the application can reflect automatically in the deployed application. Complete the following steps to configure the delivery pipeline:

1. From the application **Overview** page, as described previously, click the **Add Git Repo and Pipeline** option, as shown in the following screenshot:

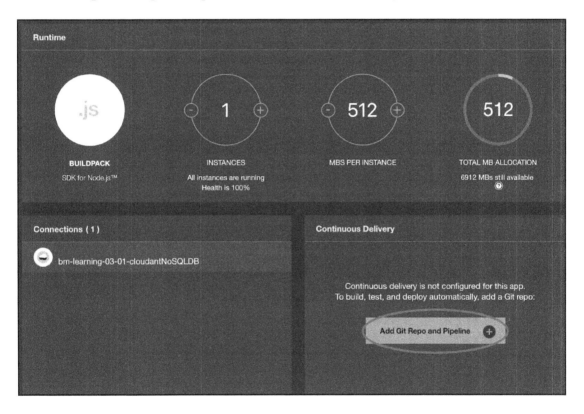

2. This will create a Git Repository for you. You will need to provide an alias to associate your IBM ID with; this alias is used in Git repository paths and so on:

3. Once your alias is created and associated with your IBM ID, click **Continue**, as shown in the following screenshot:

4. Ensure that the checkbox next to **Populate the repo with starter app package and enabe the Build & Deploy pipeline** is checked. This will populate the Git repository with the source code corresponding to this starter application:

5. It will take few seconds to create your Git repository. Once the repository is created, you will see the Git URL below the **GIT URL** option for your application repository from the **Overview** page under **Continuous Delivery**:

6. Click on the Git URL. This will take you to the Git repository for your application. You can see the source for this starter application in your repository:

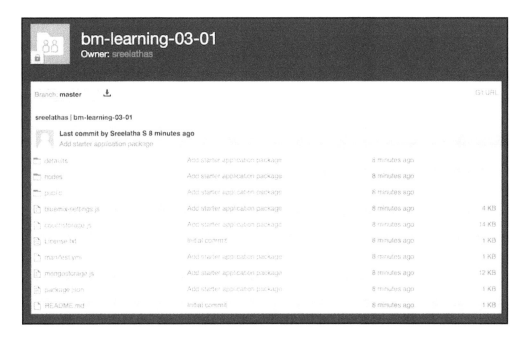

7. You can work on the source by clicking the **EDIT CODE** option. **TRACK & PLAN** can be used to configure capabilities to project manage your application. This includes creating work items, assigning and tracking them, creating agile sprint plans, and so on:

8. To configure the continuous delivery pipeline for building and deploying your application on Bluemix triggered by a source change, you can configure the delivery pipeline by clicking **BUILD & DEPLOY**. The default pipeline configured for your application is as shown in the following screenshot. You will see that a build stage and a deploy stage is configured. The deploy stage contains a deployment script, which has nothing but the cloud foundry commands (cf commands) to push the application to Bluemix:

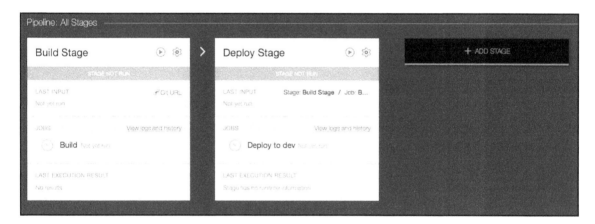

The build stage is configured to be triggered when there is a Git commit in the repository identified by the Git URL.

9. Go to **JOBS** from the screen shown in the following screenshot, to define the type of build you want to configure:

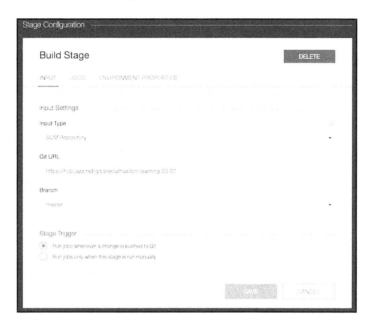

The available builder types are shown in the following screenshot:

You can configure multiple jobs within the same stage by clicking ADD JOB, as shown in following screenshot:

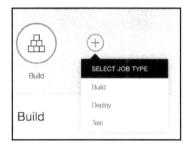

The types of jobs that you can configure within a stage are as follows:

- **Build**
- **Deploy**
- **Test**

You can use the **Test** job type to configure tests that need to be run once the build for your application completes.

You can also use **ENVIRONMENT PROPERTIES** to define properties that need to be used across your jobs from the screen, as shown in the following screenshot:

For this illustration, we will use the default pipeline configuration with one build stage using a **Simple** Builder type and one deploy stage, which will deploy the built application to a space within your organization on Bluemix. Go to the deploy stage configuration by clicking on the stage configuration icon, as shown in the following screenshot, and clicking **Configure Stage** from the pop-up menu:

The deploy stage looks like the following screenshot:

The supported deployments, as configured using the **Deployer Type** values, are as follows:

- Cloud Foundry
- Active Deploy-Begin
- Deploys using IBM Active Deploy to deploy the application to Cloud Foundry or the IBM Container service
- Active Deploy-Complete
- Deploys using IBM Active Deploy to deploy the application to Cloud Foundry on Bluemix, the IBM Container service on Bluemix, or the IBM Virtual Machines infrastructure on Bluemix
- IBM Containers on Bluemix

You can edit the push command in the deployment script of the deploy stage for your application.

You can also configure the deployment of your application to another region, organization, and space by selecting the desired **Target**, **Organization**, and **Space** at the deploy stage.

Editing the source using a web editor

You can edit the application source using any of the development editors of your choice locally, or you can also edit your application code using the web editor provided by IBM DevOps services. The web editor provided on Bluemix is based on the Eclipse Orion project:

1. To edit the starter application code, click **EDIT CODE** on the page displayed by clicking on the Git URL for your application:

2. You can navigate through your source files using the navigation on the left. Once you select the source file that you want to modify, it opens up in an editor to the right, as shown in the following screenshot:

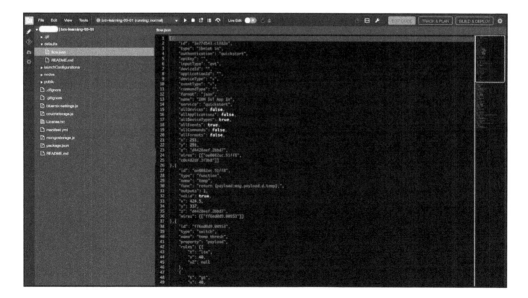

3. We will modify the `flow.json` file to illustrate the continuous delivery. Modify the template node when the temperature goes above the threshold value. Change the output from `Temperature ({{payload}}) is critical` to `Temperature ({{payload}}) is critical. You will need to take safety measures.` Click **File** | **Save**:

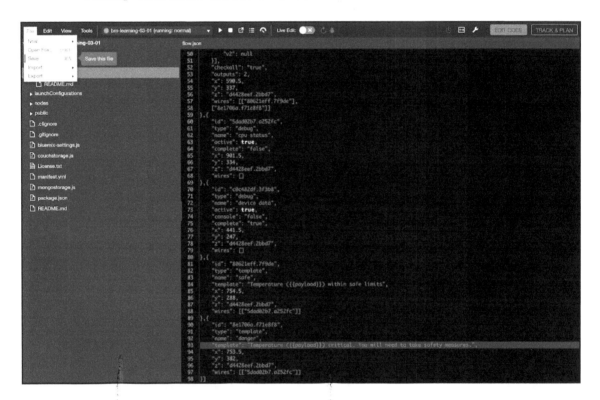

4. Click the Git icon, which is on the left-hand side of the editor, as shown in the screenshot. This will take you to the page that shows the changes to the files that you just made. You can enter a commit message in the box shown and click commit; this will make the changed file available under outgoing changes.

You can click **Push** to push your changes to the master repository:

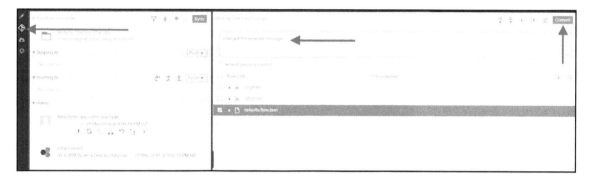

 You can also work on this Git repository using the Git command line, or other supported Git interfaces.

5. Go to **Build & Deploy** and you will see that the build stage has been triggered automatically with the source change pushed to master. Successful build has triggered the deploy stage. Successful completion of the deploy stage shows the updated application URL or route, as shown in the following screenshot:

6. To be able to view the application update that we just made, we will need to increase the temperature beyond the threshold value, which is 40 degrees centigrade, as defined in the switch node, which we saw earlier.

7. To change the temperature on the simulated device, go back to `https://quickst art.internetofthings.ibmcloud.com/iotsensor/` and increase the temperature on your device:

 Make sure the device ID is the same as the one we used earlier. If you have accidently closed the browser, you will need to note the new device ID and edit the ibmiot node in your flow to receive data from the new device ID.

8. Click the application route to view the application update, by going back your Node-RED editor and viewing the output in the debug tab.

In this section, we looked at a simple example of how to achieve continuous delivery for your application by configuring the stages in the delivery pipeline.

Extending the application

We will now look at how easy it is to extend your Node-RED application. To extend the application, we will use a **Cloudant NoSQL DB** node in flow, so that when the temperature exceeds the critical threshold, there is a database entry made in your configured Cloudant database.

Complete the following steps to extend this application:

1. Add a **Cloudant NoSQL DB** service instance using the procedure we have discussed in previous chapters to add any service instance on Bluemix.
2. Once the **Cloudant NoSQL DB** service instance is added to your Bluemix organization and space, you will see it listed in your dashboard, as shown in the following screenshot:

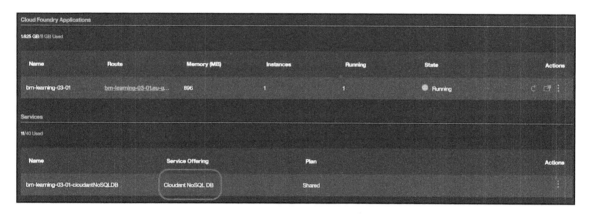

3. Go to your application route and go to the flow editor.
4. Drag and drop the cloudant node from under the storage category in the palette to your flow editor.
5. Remove the wiring of the template node named `danger` to the debug node.
6. Wire the output node of `danger` to connect to the cloudant input node.

7. Double-click on the cloudant node to configure the cloudant service instance; you will see that the service instance you have added to your Bluemix organization and space gets listed:

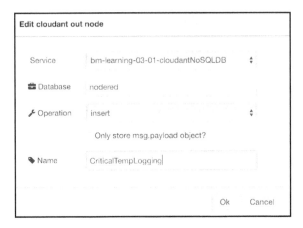

8. To configure the **Database** field, you will need to first go to the Cloudant service instance you have created and click **Launch** to launch the cloudant console. From here, you can create a new database, `nodered`. Provide the name of the database you created in the cloudant node configuration:

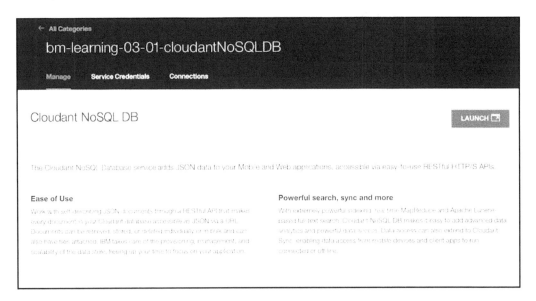

The flow for the extended application is as shown in the following diagram:

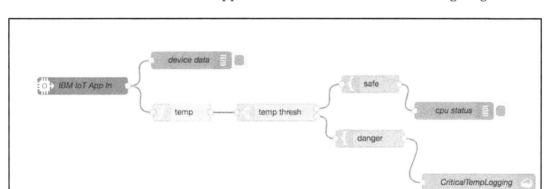

9. Click **Deploy** on the flow editor to deploy the updated application to Bluemix.
10. To check the output, ensure that the temperature in your simulated device is above the threshold value configured, which is 40 degrees centigrade.
11. Go to the Cloudant console to view the databases, query the database `nodered`. Ensure **Include Docs** is checked; you will see the entries from the `danger` node logged in to the cloudant database configured, as shown in the following screenshot:

Summary

In this chapter, we learned how to compose applications using the Node-RED editor, and how to deploy the application on Node.js runtime on Bluemix. Applications that can be composed, such as Node-RED applications, are easily extensible; the functionality of such applications can be extended by wiring additional nodes to the flow. We also looked at how to use the IBM DevOps services to configure a continuous delivery pipeline for your application. In this chapter, you also learned about how to create a Git repository for your application and how to use the web editor for working on your application source files.

In the next chapter, we will see how we can build applications on public Bluemix that leverage on-premises software.

4
Leveraging On-Premise Software for Applications on Bluemix

In this chapter, we will learn about the services on Bluemix that allow a hybrid cloud application development platform. We will learn, with an example, about how to use one of the integration services on Bluemix to connect to an application or enterprise software that is running locally on your desktop. In other words, these services are what allows for connectivity to enterprise on-premise software from the public cloud environment.

In this chapter, we will cover the following topics:

- Creating an application on Bluemix
- Adding Watson services to the application
- Installing and configuring an on-premise database
- Creating the Secure Gateway service
- Configuring the Secure Gateway service:
  - Adding Gateway
  - Adding Destination
  - Installing the Secure Gateway client
- Updating the application to use the on-premise database
- Seeing it all working together

Services under the Integrate category

Bluemix provides a set of services under the category of Integrate. These services provide the functionality to securely connect from applications on cloud to applications residing in a trusted or secure environment. To view the set of services available, follow these steps:

1. Go to the welcome page, as shown in the following screenshot, and click **Integrate**:

2. Click the icon highlighted in the following screenshot to go to the catalog of services under the **Integrate** category:

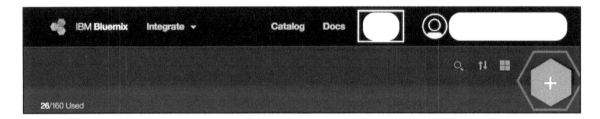

3. The services available on Bluemix, which provide the function of integrating cloud and enterprise on-premise resources, are shown in the following screenshot:

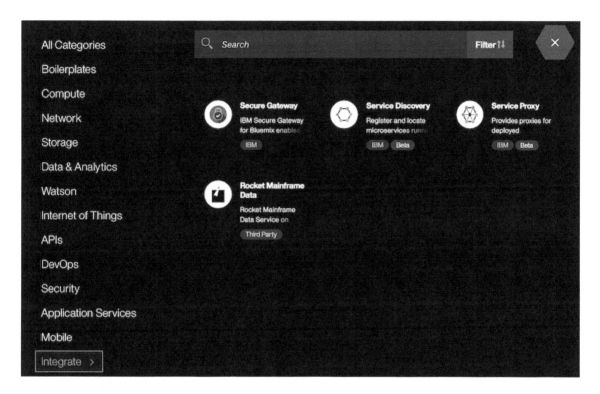

 The services shown in the preceding screenshot are those that are available at the time of writing this book.

Let us next learn how to create an application that will use an on-premise resource, such as a database, and how we can use one of the integration services on Bluemix to help achieve this. In the process of this illustration, you will also have the opportunity to be briefly introduced to the Watson set of cognitive services available on Bluemix and how they can be used in the application used for this illustration.

Creating an application on Bluemix

In this section, we will create a sample application on Bluemix by using one of the available boilerplates. For this illustration, we will be using the Node-RED boilerplate. Follow the steps to create the application:

1. Log in to Bluemix and from the welcome page, click **Compute**:

2. Click on the icon highlighted in the following screenshot to take you to the options available on Bluemix to create a Cloud Foundry application:

3. Select the **Node-RED Starter** boilerplate, as shown in the following screenshot:

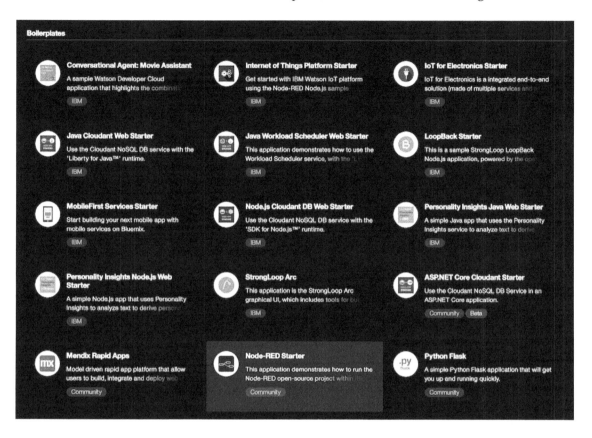

4. Give your application a name, review the plans for the services that come with the boilerplate, and click **Create**:

5. Once your application is created and started successfully, you will see it on the dashboard, as shown in the following screenshot. Click **Open URL** to go to the Node-RED editor, from where you can start wiring your application's functionality:

6. Click **Go to your Node-RED flow editor**:

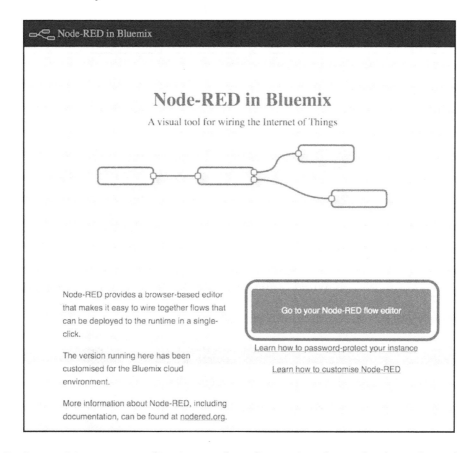

7. Start wiring your application on the editor using the nodes from the palette on the left.

For this illustration, we are going to read a Twitter feed and we are going to find the sentiment of the tweets. We are also going to translate the same tweet. We will persist all of this in the on-premise database that we will configure later in the chapter.

8. We will first wire the flow with the nodes that we need. We will then learn to configure each of these nodes individually. The flow we will wire for this application is shown as follows:

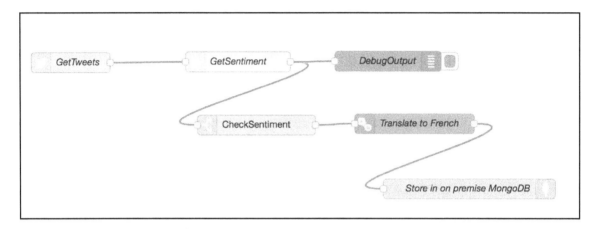

9. You can see the flow wired in the Node-RED editor, as shown in the following screenshot; also indicated in the screenshot are the different parts of the editor, which will be referred to in this chapter:

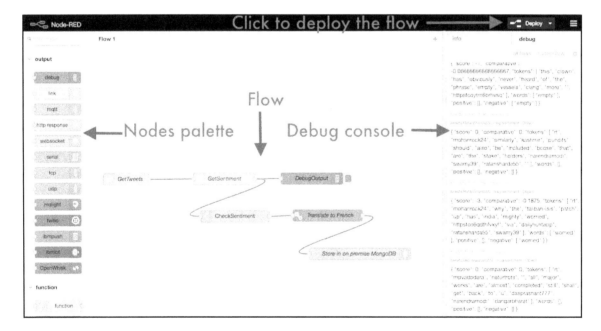

Wiring and configuring the flow

Let us learn to wire and configure the flow:

1. In your empty editor pane, drag and drop the **twitter** output node from the nodes palette:

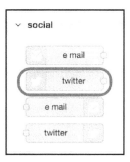

2. Configure the Twitter output node by double-clicking on the node after placing it in the editor pane. Give the node a name in the **Name** field. Add a Twitter account credential by configuring the **Twitter ID** field, clicking the pencil icon next to it. Provide a list of Twitter handles or hashtags that you would want this node to read from the Twitter stream. Click **Done** once the configuration of the node is complete:

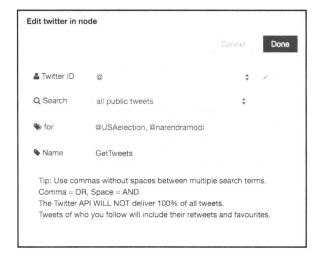

3. Next we want to analyze the sentiment of each of the tweets retrieved by the Twitter node, so let us drag and drop the sentiment node from the palette to the editor pane. Let us then wire the Twitter node and the sentiment node by clicking the endpoint on the Twitter node and dragging it to connect to the endpoint on the sentiment node:

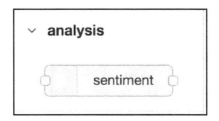

4. To configure the sentiment node, double-click on it and give it a name, as shown in the following screenshot:

5. Next we need to check on the value of the sentiment score of each tweet to make a decision to only work on those tweets that express a negative sentiment. The sentiment node will analyze the content of each tweet and will output a JSON file, which has what is called the sentiment score, and other details, such as what is shown in the following code, for an example tweet:

```
{
  "score": -9,
  "comparative": -0.36,
  "tokens": [
    "rt", "pmoindia", "saddened", "by", "the", "loss", "of",
    "lives", "due", "to", "a", "quake", "in", "italy",
    "condolences", "to", "bereaved", "families", "amp", "prayers",
    "with", "those", "injured", "pm", "nar"],
  "words": ["injured", "bereaved", "loss", "saddened"],
    "positive": [],
    "negative": ["injured", "bereaved", "loss", "saddened"]
}
```

6. We will use the value of the score in the sentiment analysis response to check whether the sentiment was negative, as in our application, we only want to persist negative tweets. For this, let us add a **switch** node:

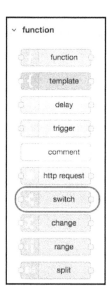

7. Double-click on the node to configure it. Give the node a name and change the property you want to monitor to **msg.sentiment.score**. Add a rule that checks for this property value to be less than 0, if true; it would mean that the tweet had a negative sentiment and that we would need to send it to the next part of the flow, where we are going to do some more augmentation and write the tweets to a persistent store, such as a database:

You can add an additional rule to check whether the sentiment score value is greater than 0; if true, you can wire any other appropriate action on such tweets. For this illustration, we will ignore tweets with positive and neutral sentiments.

8. Next let us drag and drop the **language translation** node from under the Watson category of nodes in the palette:

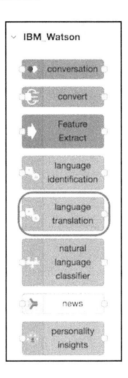

Before we can configure the language translation node, we will need to add the related Watson service to the Bluemix space. Follow the steps to add the Watson service for language translation:

1. In your Bluemix dashboard, from the welcome page, click on the **Watson** category, as shown in the following screenshot:

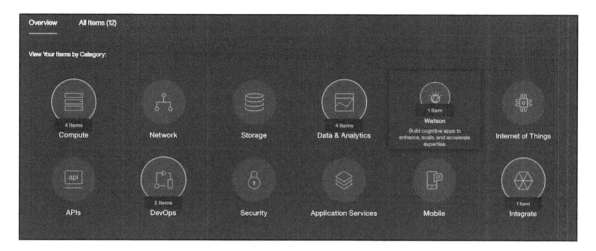

2. Click on the icon shown in the following screenshot to see the catalog of **Watson** services:

3. From the list of available services, click the **Language Translator** service:

4. Review the information about the service and service plan, and click **Create**:

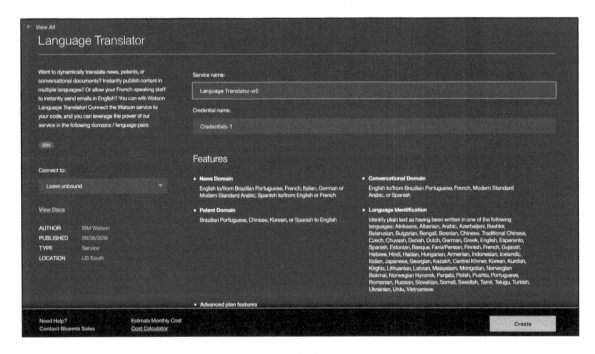

5. Once the service is created, you will be taken to the **Manage** screen, as shown in the following screenshot:

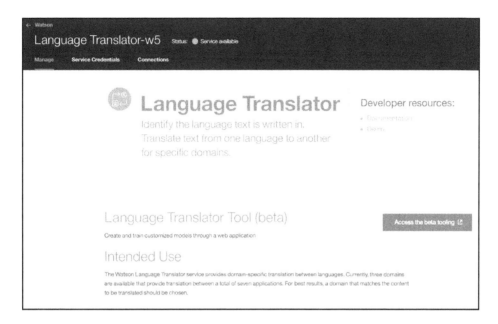

6. Go to the **Service Credentials** tab; you will see one credential created for the service. You can click on **View Credentials**. Make a note of the username and password; we will need them when we configure the language translation node in the Node-RED editor:

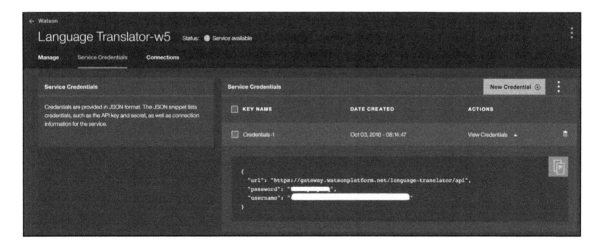

Now let us go back to the Node-RED editor for our application where we just added a language translation node. Let us now continue to wire and configure our application.

7. Double-click the language translation node and configure it as shown in the following screenshot. Enter the username and password that you obtained in the previous step. Give the node a name. Choose the **Target** language you want to translate the content to. For this illustration, we will choose **French**. Click **Done** once you complete the configuration:

8. We can also add a debug node from the output nodes category to see the output of the sentiment node in the debug console. If you want to see the payload, choose **Output** as **msg.payload**; if you want to only see the sentiment, you can choose **Output** to be **msg.sentiment**, as shown in the following screenshot:

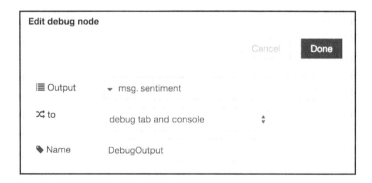

9. Drag and drop the **mongodb** node from under the **storage** category. Our application will persist the translated tweets in MongoDB:

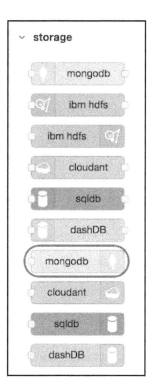

Before we can configure the MongoDB node, we will need to complete a couple of things. Firstly, since we are going to be using an on-premise database for this illustration, we will need to download and install MongoDB locally. Secondly, since we need to establish connectivity from a public cloud to an on-premise environment, we will need to add and configure the integration service on Bluemix; we will be using the Secure Gateway service.

Downloading and installing MongoDB

To install MongoDB locally, you can download the latest version of MongoDB for your operating system from `https://www.mongodb.com/download-center`. You can download the Community Server version. In this illustration, we will be showing the screenshots as applicable to Mac OS.

Starting the MongoDB daemon and working with MongoDB

Once you have installed MongoDB, follow these steps to start the MongoDB daemon:

1. Create the `data/db` folder structure under the user's `home` directory.

2. Open the terminal window (or command prompt if your OS is Windows) and go to the folder where MongoDB is installed. Change directory to `/bin` and execute the following command:

   `./mongod --dbpath ~/data/db`

3. This starts the MongoDB daemon. The following screenshot shows the output on the terminal window. Note the port number at which it is listening for connections:

```
                                         bin — mongod --dbpath ~/data/db — 169×55
                                :$ ./mongod --dbpath ~/data/db
2016-10-04T17:01:15.895+0530 I CONTROL  [initandlisten] MongoDB starting : pid=5187 port=27017 dbpath=/Users/          'data/db 64-bit host=          -MacBook-Pro.local
2016-10-04T17:01:15.896+0530 I CONTROL  [initandlisten] db version v3.2.8
2016-10-04T17:01:15.896+0530 I CONTROL  [initandlisten] git version: ed70e33130c977bda0024c125b56d159573dbaf0
2016-10-04T17:01:15.896+0530 I CONTROL  [initandlisten] OpenSSL version: OpenSSL 0.9.8zh 14 Jan 2016
2016-10-04T17:01:15.896+0530 I CONTROL  [initandlisten] allocator: system
2016-10-04T17:01:15.896+0530 I CONTROL  [initandlisten] modules: none
2016-10-04T17:01:15.896+0530 I CONTROL  [initandlisten] build environment:
2016-10-04T17:01:15.896+0530 I CONTROL  [initandlisten]     distarch: x86_64
2016-10-04T17:01:15.896+0530 I CONTROL  [initandlisten]     target_arch: x86_64
2016-10-04T17:01:15.896+0530 I CONTROL  [initandlisten] options: { storage: { dbPath: "/Users/          /data/db" } }
2016-10-04T17:01:15.897+0530 I -        [initandlisten] Detected data files in /Users/:          ./data/db created by the 'wiredTiger' storage engine, so setting the activ
e storage engine to 'wiredTiger'.
2016-10-04T17:01:15.898+0530 I STORAGE  [initandlisten] wiredtiger_open config: create,cache_size=4G,session_max=20000,eviction=(threads_max=4),config_base=false,statist
ics=(fast),log=(enabled=true,archive=true,path=journal,compressor=snappy),file_manager=(close_idle_time=100000),checkpoint=(wait=60,log_size=2GB),statistics_log=(wait=0)
,
2016-10-04T17:01:16.757+0530 I CONTROL  [initandlisten]
2016-10-04T17:01:16.757+0530 I CONTROL  [initandlisten] ** WARNING: soft rlimits too low. Number of files is 256, should be at least 1000
2016-10-04T17:01:16.821+0530 I NETWORK  [HostnameCanonicalizationWorker] Starting hostname canonicalization worker
2016-10-04T17:01:16.821+0530 I FTDC     [initandlisten] Initializing full-time diagnostic data capture with directory '/Users/:          /data/db/diagnostic.data'
2016-10-04T17:01:16.825+0530 I NETWORK  [initandlisten] waiting for connections on port 27017
```

4. Let us open a new terminal window and change directory to `/bin` under the MongoDB installation directory. This starts the MongoDB shell, where you will see the following terminal output. This is where you can start executing MongoDB commands:

```
            -MacBook-Pro:bin .          $ ./mongo
MongoDB shell version: 3.2.8
connecting to: test
Welcome to the MongoDB shell.
For interactive help, type "help".
For more comprehensive documentation, see
        http://docs.mongodb.org/
Questions? Try the support group
        http://groups.google.com/group/mongodb-user
Server has startup warnings:
2016-08-23T18:36:57.917+0530 I CONTROL  [initandlisten]
2016-08-23T18:36:57.917+0530 I CONTROL  [initandlisten] ** WARNING: soft rlimits too low. Number of files is 256, should be at least 1000
```

5. Let us create a database for our application; we will call it `mydb`. Execute the following MongoDB command from the Mongo shell to create and switch to the new database:

```
use mydb
```

6. Create a collection by using the following command:

```
db.translatedtweets.insert({"SampleTweet" : "Example for a tweet"})
```

7. Make a note of the IP address of the host machine where this MongoDB instance is installed.

With this, we have installed and set up a local MongoDB instance for use by our application. Let us now move on to the next important set of steps, where we will see how to add and configure the Secure Gateway integration service on Bluemix, which will provide the critical secure pipe between the public cloud and on-premise environments, enabling us to have a hybrid cloud application development environment.

Creating the Secure Gateway service instance

Let us now learn how to create the Secure Gateway service instance on Bluemix. Follow these steps to do this:

1. Go to the welcome page, as shown in the following screenshot, and click **Integrate**:

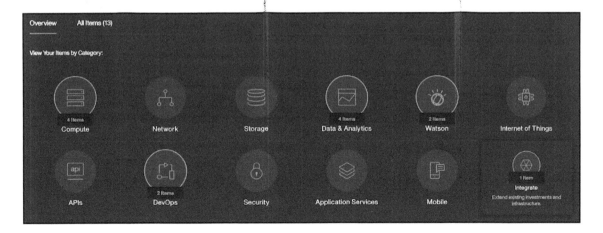

2. Click the icon highlighted in the following screenshot to go to the catalog of services under the **Integrate** category:

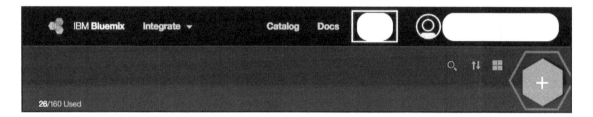

3. Click **Secure Gateway**:

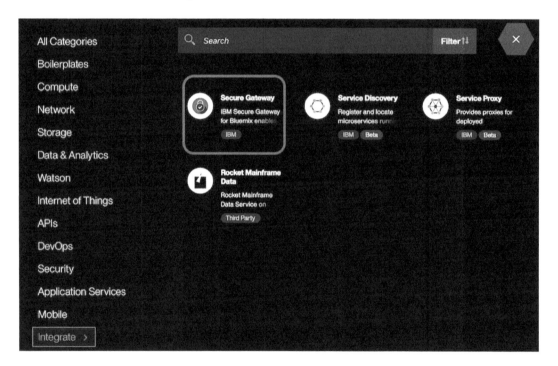

4. Review the details of the service and click**Create**.

Once the service is created, you can click on the service tile on the Bluemix dashboard to configure it.

Configuring the Secure Gateway service instance

To configure the secure gateway service to create a gateway to your MongoDB destination, follow these steps:

1. Click on the **Secure Gateway** service tile from the dashboard:

2. In the Secure Gateway dashboard, under the **Manage** section, click **Add Gateway**, as shown in the following screenshot, to first add a gateway:

3. Give a name to the gateway, uncheck the **Require security token to connect clients** and **Token Expiration** options, and click **ADD GATEWAY**:

4. The gateway is now added, as shown in the following screenshot. Click on this new gateway, **mymongo**, to add **Destinations**:

5. Click **Add Destination** to add a new destination to the gateway you created. Select **On-Premises**, as shown in the following screenshot, then click **Next**:

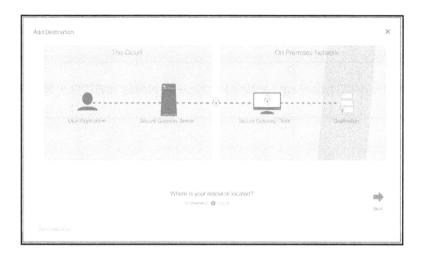

6. Enter the hostname or IP address of the machine where you have locally installed MongoDB. Provide the port number where your MongoDB is listening for connections. We obtained a port number earlier when we started the MongoDB daemon. Once done, click **Next**:

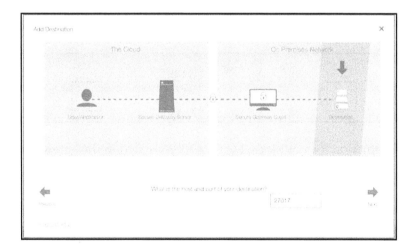

7. Choose the protocol as **TCP**. Click **Next**:

8. Select the destination authentication type as **None**, then click **Next**:

9. For this illustration, we will not be configuring an IP table, so click **Next** without making any changes in the screen as shown here:

10. Give a name to the destination you are going to create. Click **Finish**:

11. The destination for your local MongoDB is created in the gateway, as shown in the following screenshot:

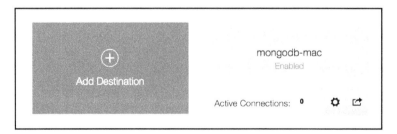

12. Let us now install the secure gateway client on the local machine where MongoDB is installed. Make a note of your **gateway ID**, as shown in the following screenshot. Click **Add Client** to start the installation of the secure gateway client:

13. There are three different ways you can install and configure the secure gateway client. You can use a direct installation of the client by downloading the client installable for your operating system from this screen, as shown here:

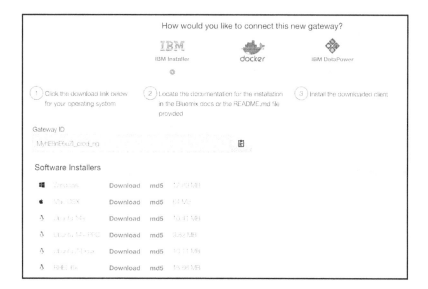

14. For this illustration, we will use the second option, which is by using Docker. As a pre-requisite for the next set of steps, you will need to download and install Docker for your operating system. You can refer to `https://www.docker.com/products/docker` for the installable and installation instructions.

15. Once you have Docker installed locally, you can launch the Docker QuickStart Terminal (in Mac) or the boot2docker, based on your operating system, to start Docker.

16. Run the following command in the Docker terminal:

```
docker pull ibmcom/secure-gateway-client
```

This is required to get the latest version of the secure gateway client image. You will see something like the following in the Docker terminal window:

```
Docker is up and running!
To see how to connect your Docker Client to the Docker Engine running on this virtual machine, run: /usr/local/bin/docker-machine
env default


                        ##         .
                  ## ## ##        ==
               ## ## ## ## ##    ===
           /""""""""""""""""""\___/ ===
      ~~~ {~~ ~~~~ ~~~ ~~~~ ~~ ~ /  ===- ~~~
           _____ o           __/
             \    \         __/
              _____/


docker is configured to use the default machine with IP 192.     .100
For help getting started, check out the docs at https://docs.docker.com

.        ;-MacBook-Pro:user-folder           $ docker pull ibmcom/secure-gateway-client
Using default tag: latest
latest: Pulling from ibmcom/secure-gateway-client

6fd1c5075c0a: Pull complete
5ab429cc7c71: Pull complete
be3a4724bfdf: Pull complete
998426d0362f: Pull complete
a3ed95caeb02: Pull complete
Digest: sha256:2d2f097ec89c35e41f37739572c0b61ff7186bde6c80993320733ab2e62eb044
Status: Downloaded newer image for ibmcom/secure-gateway-client:latest
```

17. Next run the following Docker command to start the container with the secure gateway client:

```
docker run -it ibmcom/secure-gateway-client <Gateway ID>
```

18. Replace the gateway ID with the gateway ID value indicated in the screenshot for Step 12.

You should get the results, as shown in the following screenshot:

```
          -MacBook-Pro:user-folder              $ docker run -it ibmcom/secure-gateway-client XqtirvW7DB2_prod_ng
IBM Bluemix Secure Gateway Client Version 1.5.1
********************************************************************************************
You  are running the  IBM Secure  Gateway Client for Bluemix. When you enter the provided docker
command the IBM Secure Gateway Client  for Bluemix automatically downloads as a Docker image and
is executed on your system/device. This is released under an IBM license. The  license agreement
for IBM  Secure Gateway Client for Bluemix is available at the following location:

http://www.ibm.com/software/sla/sladb.nsf/lilookup/986C7686F22D4D3585257E13004EA6CB?OpenDocument

Your use of the components of the package and  dependencies constitutes your acceptance  of this
license agreement. If you do  not want to accept the license, immediately quit  the container by
closing  the  terminal  window or by  entering 'quit' followed by  the ENTER key. Then, delete any
pulled Docker image from your device.

For client documentation, please view the ReadMe located at:
.rpm and .deb installers: /opt/ibm/securegateway/docs/
.dmg installer:           <installation location>/ibm/securegateway/docs/
.exe installer:           <installation location>\Secure Gateway Client\ibm\securegateway\docs\
********************************************************************************************


<press enter for the command line>
[2016-08-24 02:02:19.747] [INFO] (Client ID 1) No password provided. The UI will not require a password for access
[2016-08-24 02:02:19.782] [WARN] (Client ID 1) UI Server started. The UI is not currently password protected
[2016-08-24 02:02:19.783] [INFO] (Client ID 1) Visit localhost:9003/dashboard to view the UI.
[2016-08-24 02:02:20.062] [INFO] (Client ID 10) Setting log level to INFO
[2016-08-24 02:02:22.872] [INFO] (Client ID 10) The Secure Gateway tunnel is connected
[2016-08-24 02:02:23.497] [INFO] (Client ID XqtirvW7DB2_Pgx) Your Client ID is XqtirvW7DB2_Pgx
XqtirvW7DB2_Pgx>
```

19. To make sure you have the right permissions in the ACL to connect to your MongoDB instance, run the following command from the Docker terminal:

```
acl allow <Hostname or IP address>:<Port>
```

The following screenshot shows the command on the terminal:

```
[XqtirvW7DB2_Pgx> acl allow 9.:          :.147:27017
```

Once the secure gateway client is up and running, you will see the status reflected in the secure gateway client configuration screen. You will see that your gateway is now connected to the remote resource, which is your local MongoDB instance:

You can also see the status on your gateway details screen, as shown in the following screenshot:

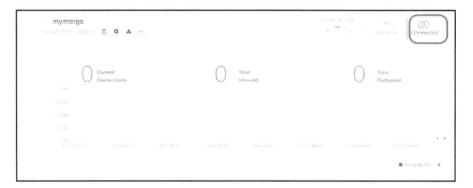

20. Click the gear icon in your destination to view its details:

21. This opens the destination details, as shown in the following screenshot. Make a note of the **Cloud Host : Port** value; this will be required when we configure the MongoDB node in our application, in the Node-RED editor:

Having completed the configuration of the Secure Gateway service instance to connect to your on-premise MongoDB database, you can now resume editing your application from where we left off.

22. Go back to the Node-RED editor for your application and double-click on the MongoDB node to configure it. Give the node a name. Provide the name of the collection that we created earlier, using the Mongo shell, in the **Collection** field. Select the **insert** operation. Check the checkbox for **Only store msg.payload object**. To configure the MongoDB server details, click on the pencil icon next to the **Server** field, as highlighted in the following screenshot. Click **Done** when the configuration is complete:

23. In the **Server** configuration, provide the **Cloud Host : Port** value which was obtained from Step 20, provide these as the MongoDB server host and port in the Server configuration for the MongoDB node, as shown in the following screenshot:

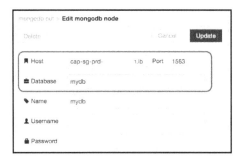

24. Now you have finished wiring the Node-RED application. You can deploy the completed flow to Bluemix by clicking Deploy, as shown in Node-RED editor screenshot in Step 11 of the *Creating an application on Bluemix* section.

25. To verify whether your application is able to connect to your on-premise MongoDB database and insert translated Twitter data carrying negative sentiments, you can go back to your Mongo shell and execute the following command:

```
db.translatedtweets.find()
```

26. You will see the tweets carrying negative sentiments and translated in French, fetched from your local MongoDB database, as shown here:

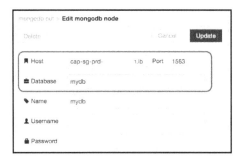

Summary

In this chapter, we learned how to build an application that leverages on-premise resources. We learned how to use the Secure Gateway integration service to achieve the secure connectivity to the on-premise MongoDB database from your application hosted on Bluemix, which is a public cloud. In this way, we saw how Bluemix provides a hybrid cloud application development environment.

In the following chapter, we will learn how to scale the applications deployed on Bluemix manually, or by using the related DevOps services provided on Bluemix.

5
Scaling Applications in Bluemix

In the previous chapter, we learned how to integrate applications deployed on Bluemix with software that is deployed on-premise. In this chapter, we will look at what capabilities are available in Bluemix to allow users to scale the applications deployed on Bluemix. We will learn to configure scaling policies on an application deployed on Bluemix, such that the application scales when under load. To begin with, we will try to understand what it means when we say scaling, and what types of scaling are possible. This chapter will cover the following topics:

- Overview of scaling types supported in Bluemix
- Creating an application that can scale
- Configuring a load test for the application
- Manually scaling your application
- Scaling your application using the Auto-Scaling service in Bluemix:
- Creating the Auto-Scaling service instance
- Binding the Auto-Scaling service to your application
- Defining the scaling policy for your application

Overview of scaling types supported in Bluemix

Building scalable applications has become the de facto standard for modern web applications. Applications need to be built to scale. Scaling of applications is required when there is a need to meet increased activity within the application. Applications that scale are highly available and responsive to requests. There are two types of scaling, as follows:

- Vertical scaling
- Horizontal scaling

Vertical scaling

When applications are deployed, they use compute resources to run. These compute resources are:

- CPU (processing)
- RAM (memory)

Scaling applications by increasing the resources available to them in the same machine or physical node is called vertical scaling; this is also known as *scaling up*. This method of scaling is useful for applications that are designed and developed in such a way that they cannot share state or data. Less modular applications, or applications with more tightly coupled modules, usually have a need to scale within the same node or physical machine. By vertically scaling these applications, there are more resources that are attached to, or made available to, the application for use when there is an increase in load on the application.

The flip side to vertical scaling is that the applications become a single point of failure, which means that if there is a disruption to the physical node where the application resides then the entire application becomes unavailable until the physical machine is restored.

The following figure shows an illustration of what scaling up, or vertical scaling, is:

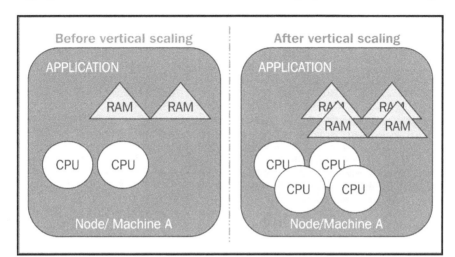

Horizontal scaling

Horizontal scaling is also called *scaling out*. Unlike vertical scaling, in horizontal scaling, resources are added to the application by scaling the application out to another node or physical machine. The application that is scaled out to a new node gets the same set of resources to work with. To use this scaling technique, it is important that the applications are designed in such a way that the state and application data are shared across the nodes. This makes it necessary for application design to externalize data stored in memory or local file systems. Also, when applications are scaled out, it becomes necessary to have a load balancer in front of the nodes so that the application requests are routed, based on routing policies defined in the load balancer, to application instances or nodes.

The advantage of horizontal scaling over vertical scaling is that horizontal scaling does not deplete the resources of a single physical machine or node. Also, by scaling out, the issue of **SPOF (single point of failure)** is reduced, so applications that are designed to scale horizontally are more available and have a better failover than applications that are designed to scale vertically.

The following figure shows an illustration of the horizontal scaling, or scaling out, of an application:

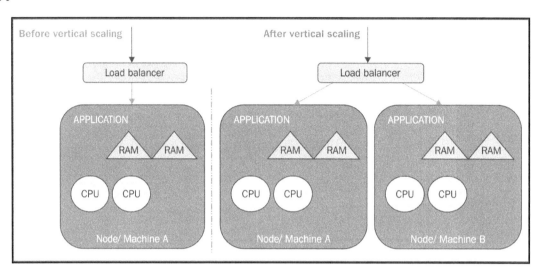

While developing cloud-native applications, it is important to consider the nature of deployment on cloud. Most of the compute capacity provided on a cloud environment such as Bluemix are transient in nature, which means that an application restart or restage does not guarantee its deployment using the same set of resources. This makes it necessary for applications that are developed as cloud-native to be designed in such a way that the state between the application modules or the application data are stored in persistent stores and not kept in memory or in local file storage.

In Bluemix, it is recommended that application data is persisted in external data stores, preferably using one of the data services available in Bluemix. For persisting application state between requests, such as for session objects, it is recommended to use the **Session Cache** service on Bluemix. For persisting data that can be accessed easily and frequently, to give an improved performance for your web application, instead of having to go to databases or data stores each time, it is recommended to use the **Data Cache** service on Bluemix:

From the dashboard shown in the preceding screenshot, you can click **Get started now!** to view the services in the Bluemix catalog. Go to the **Application Services** category to view the **Session Cache** and **Data Cache** services:

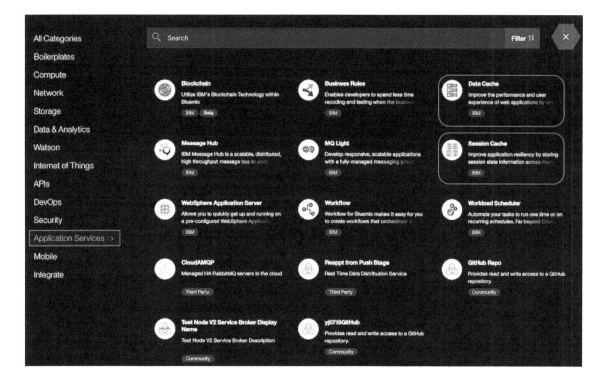

For details on working with Session Cache, you can refer to `https://ibm.biz/BdrH8h`. To learn how to use the Data Cache service, you can refer to `https://ibm.biz/BdrH83`.

Creating an application to scale on Bluemix

We will use the Java Cloudant Web Starter boilerplate to create an application, which we will use to demonstrate the scaling capabilities in Bluemix:

1. From the Bluemix dashboard, go to the **Compute** option and click on **Get started now!**, as shown in the following screenshot:

2. Select the **Java Cloudant Web Starter** boilerplate:

Boilerplates

Conversational Agent: Movie Assistant

A sample Watson Developer Cloud application that highlights the

IBM

Internet of Things Platform Starter

Get started with IBM Watson IoT platform using the Node-RED Node.js sample

IBM

IoT for Electronics Starter

IoT for Electronics is a integrated end-to-end solution (made of multiple servic

IBM

Java Cloudant Web Starter

Use the Cloudant NoSQL DB service with the 'Liberty for Java™' runtime.

IBM

Java Workload Scheduler Web Starter

This application demonstrates how to use the Workload Scheduler service, wit

IBM

LoopBack Starter

This is a sample StrongLoop LoopBack Node.js application, powered by the

IBM

MobileFirst Services Starter

Start building your next mobile app with mobile services on Bluemix.

IBM

Node.js Cloudant DB Web Starter

Use the Cloudant NoSQL DB service with the 'SDK for Node.js™' runtime.

IBM

Personality Insights Java Web Starter

A simple Java app that uses the Personality Insights service to analyz

IBM

Personality Insights Node.js Web Starter

A simple Node.js app that uses Personality Insights to analyze text t

IBM

StrongLoop Arc

This application is the StrongLoop Arc graphical UI, which includes tools fo

IBM

ASP.NET Core Cloudant Starter

Use the Cloudant NoSQL DB Service in an ASP.NET Core application.

Community   Beta

Mendix Rapid Apps

Model driven rapid app platform that allow users to build, integrate and de

Community

Node-RED Starter

This application demonstrates how to run the Node-RED open-source project

Community   Beta

Python Flask

A simple Python Flask application that will get you up and running quickly.

Community

Ruby Sinatra

Develop a Ruby web application using the Sinatra framework

Vaadin Rich Web Starter

This application demonstrates how to use the Vaadin UI Framework to build rich

3. Provide a name for your application. In this demo, the application name is `scalingdemo-b05307`. Leave the other fields with their default values, as shown in the following screenshot:

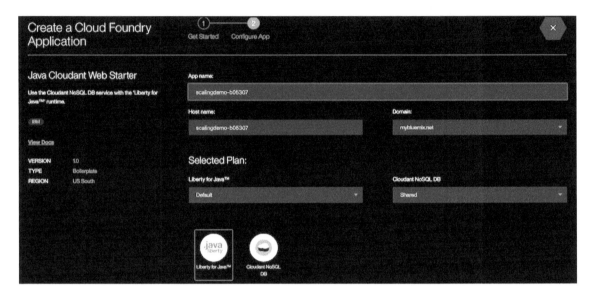

4. Click **Create**. This creates the starter application.

Configuring a load test for your application

Before we learn about the scaling options on Bluemix, let us go ahead and create a load-test scenario for the application we just created. This is required to simulate the conditions for the application where the application would need to scale.

Creating the BlazeMeter service instance

We will use the **BlazeMeter** service to configure the load-test scenario:

1. From the Bluemix catalog, select **BlazeMeter** from the **DevOps** category of services, as shown in the following screenshot:

2. Click **BlazeMeter** and review the details of the service and the service plan:

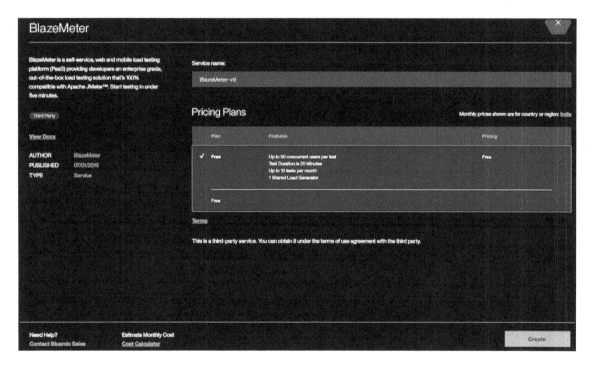

3. Click **Create**. A BlazeMeter service instance is created:

Creating the load test

Using the next set of steps, we will create a load test using the BlazeMeter service:

1. Click **OPEN BLAZEMETER DASHBOARD** to open the BlazeMeter dashboard. Click **Skip wizard**, as shown in the following screenshot:

2. From the BlazeMeter dashboard, click **Create Test**:

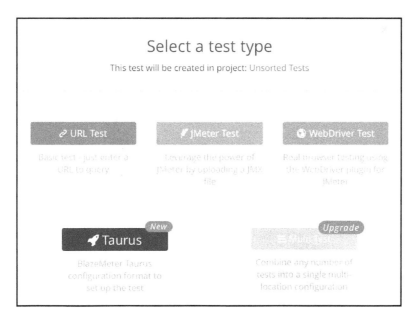

3. Click **URL Test** to create HTTP requests to your application simulating the user base and defining the time interval between requests:

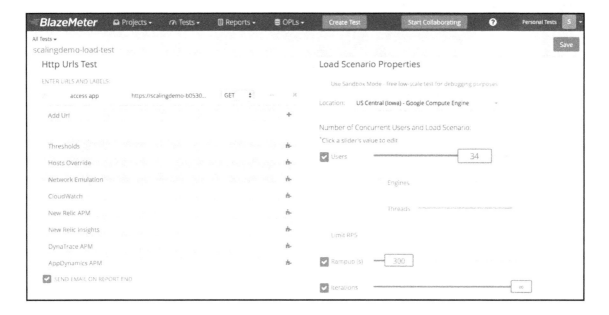

4. Click **Save**. The load test for your application is created. You can run this test to simulate a load for your application.

 To learn more about BlazeMeter, you can refer to `http://bit.ly/29P9ug E.`

Manually scaling your application

In the application's **Overview** page, you will see the number of instances and the memory allocated to each instance where your application runs:

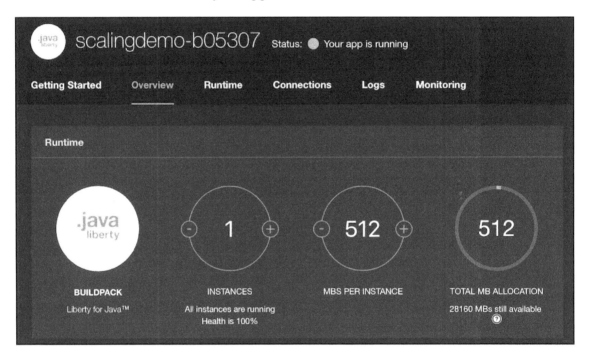

Let us now learn how to manually scale the application on Bluemix. The following are the steps to scale your application manually:

1. Click the + icon next to the instances to increase the number of instances where your application runs:

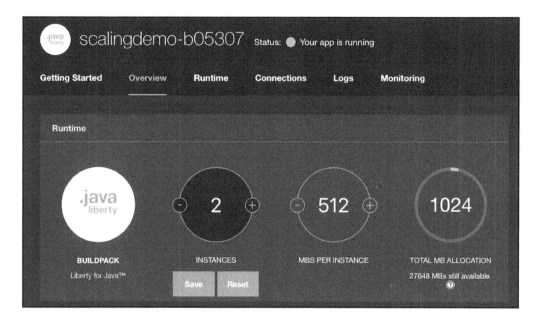

2. Click **Save**, to save the configuration:

Using manual scaling, you can increase the resources attached to your application by increasing the number of instances in which your application runs. Bluemix internally scales out or horizontally scales your application when the number of instances is increased. Bluemix has an internal load balancer, which handles the routing of requests to your application across the instances. You can also choose to scale your application by increasing the memory each instance will have. This is how you can scale your applications manually, in Bluemix.

View the activity log on the Bluemix dashboard to see the application scale out under load; you will see the information shown in the following screenshot:

To verify the application scaling, you can run load tests using the BlazeMeter service we created earlier, or you can run load tests using **JMeter**.

Scaling your application using the Auto-Scaling service in Bluemix

In the previous section, we learned how to scale our application manually. In this section, we will learn about scaling applications automatically by using the Auto-Scaling service in Bluemix.

Creating the Auto-Scaling service instance

The following are the steps to create the Auto-Scaling instance:

1. From the Bluemix catalog, select **Auto-Scaling** from the **DevOps** category of services, as shown in the following screenshot:

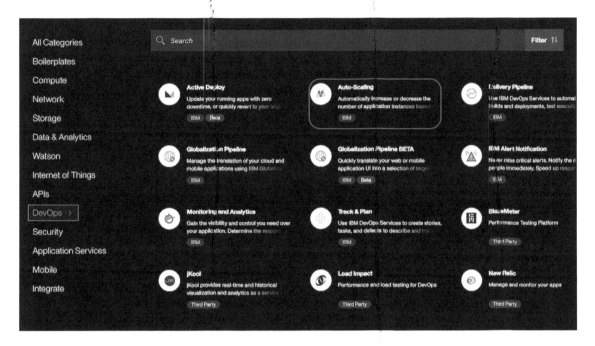

2. Click the **Auto-Scaling** service, review the service details, and click **Create**:

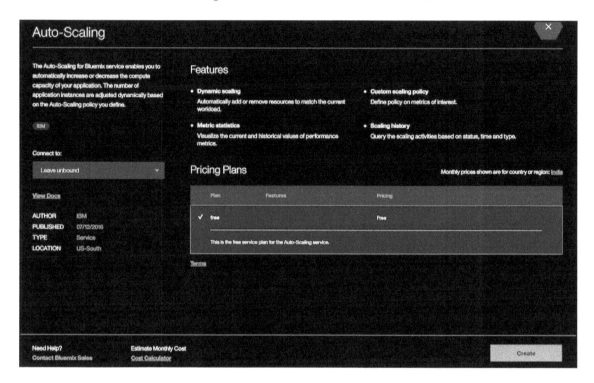

3. The **Auto-Scaling** service is created. Since we have not yet bound the application to this service, you will see the message shown in the following screenshot:

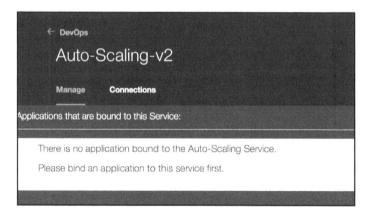

Binding the Auto-Scaling service instance to your application

Let us now bind the Auto-Scaling service to the application that we want to scale automatically using the Auto-Scaling service:

1. Go to the application details page and click **Connections**:

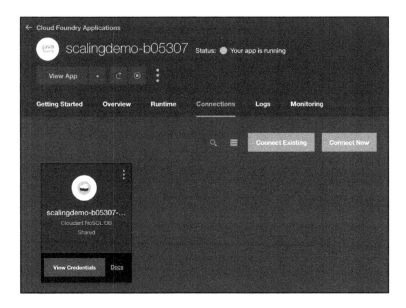

2. Click **Connect Existing.** The services that exist in your Bluemix space is displayed. Select the Auto-Scaling service instance that we just created:

3. Click **Connect**. You will be prompted to restage the application. Click **Restage**. The Auto-Scaling service instance is now bound to your application, as shown here:

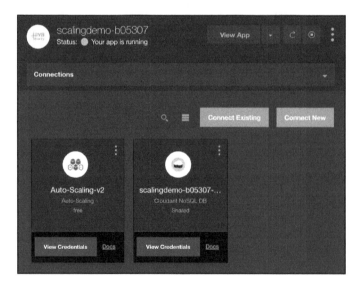

Defining the scaling policy for your application

Let us now learn how to use the Auto-Scaling service to define scaling policy, which will be used to monitor and automatically scale your application:

1. Open the Auto-Scaling dashboard by clicking the service tile from under the **Connections** view of your application details page:

2. Click **CREATE AUTO-SCALING POLICY** to create the scaling policy for your application. As shown in the following screenshot, the policy is defined based on the metrics selected from the **Metric Type** dropdown. The metric selected is **ResponseTime**. You can configure the maximum number of instances the application should scale out to. Using the policy, you can also define the scale-in condition, which would release resources when the metric that is monitored is within the desired limit.

The other metrics that can be monitored are **Memory**, **Throughput**, and **Heap**:

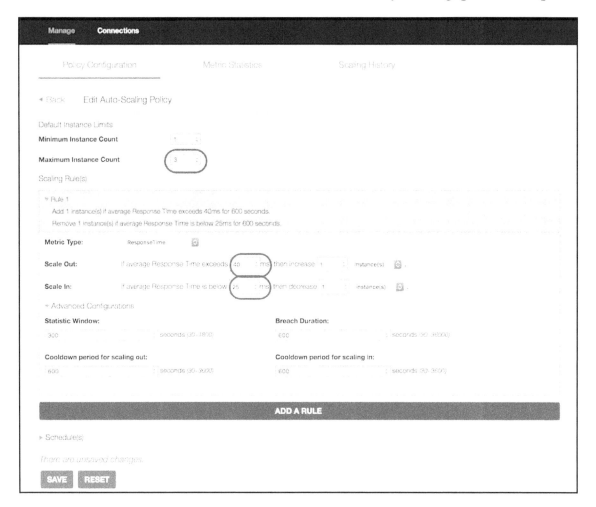

3. Click **SAVE** to save the scaling policy for your application.
4. You can also edit the scaling policy to add more than one rule by clicking on **ADD RULE**. You can change the metric type on the policy to define different conditions for your application, under which it should scale out.
5. Click **Metric Statistics** on the Auto-Scaling service dashboard to view the metrics status when your application is under load. The following is the screenshot of the memory metric for your application when it is being monitored for the rule for the memory metric. You can set the upper and lower threshold values to be the ones that you would have defined in the policy.

6. You can run the load tests using the BlazeMeter service. You can look at the load test reports from the BlazeMeter dashboard:

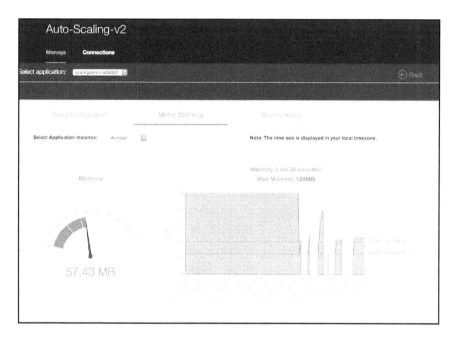

7. Click the **Scaling History** tab on the Auto-Scaling dashboard to see the scaling logs for your application.

Summary

In this chapter, you learned about application scaling. You also learned about the scaling options supported on Bluemix. Having followed the examples in this chapter, you have learned to configure the Auto-Scaling service to automatically scale your applications on Bluemix.

In the following chapter, you will learn how to use the monitoring and management capabilities on Bluemix to monitor your application.

6
Monitoring and Management in Bluemix

In this chapter, we will look at the services available in Bluemix that will users to monitor and manage the applications deployed on the platform. We will also learn how to use the monitoring and management services in Bluemix.

In this chapter, you will learn how to use some of these available monitoring and management services to monitor various parameters of your application in Bluemix.

This chapter will cover the following:

- Overview of monitoring and management services in Bluemix
- Monitoring and analytics service:
    - Creating the Monitoring and Analytics service instance
    - Creating an application to monitor using the M&A service
    - Binding the M&A service to your application
    - Simulating events in your application
    - Viewing reports in the M&A dashboard for your monitored application
- New Relic service:
    - Creating the New Relic service instance
    - Binding the New Relic service to your application
    - Configuring the application to send events to the New Relic service
    - Simulating events in your application
    - Viewing reports in the New Relic dashboard for your monitored application

Overview of monitoring and management services in Bluemix

 Discussions in this chapter will be based upon the services that are available in Bluemix at the time of writing this book (July 2016).

Some of the services that can be used to monitor and manage your applications on Bluemix are the following:

- **Monitoring and Analytics**, which is an IBM service
- **New Relic**, a third-party service
- **JKool**, a third-party service
- **IBM Alert Notification**, which is an IBM service

When you log in to Bluemix, and select **All Items**, you will see **Get started now!**, as shown in the following screenshot:

From here you can click **Get started now!** to view the services in the Bluemix catalog. Go to the **DevOps** category to view the monitoring and management services:

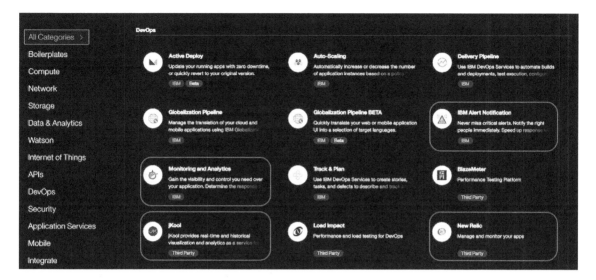

Let us now look in detail at how to use the Monitoring and Analytics service with your application in Bluemix.

Monitoring and Analytics service

Using the **Monitoring and Analytics** (**M&A**) service, you can get the details on the performance, availability and log analytics details for your application. In this section, we will learn how to create the service instance and how to configure it to enable monitoring of your application.

 M&A service is currently only supported for Java applications on Liberty Application Server and NodeJS applications.

Creating the Monitoring and Analytics service instance

When you log in to Bluemix, and select **All Items**, you will see **Get started now!** From here you can click **Get started now!** to view the services in the Bluemix catalog. Once you are in the Bluemix catalog, you can perform the following steps to create the M&A service instance:

1. In the catalog, filter the services by typing `Monitoring and Analytics` as shown here:

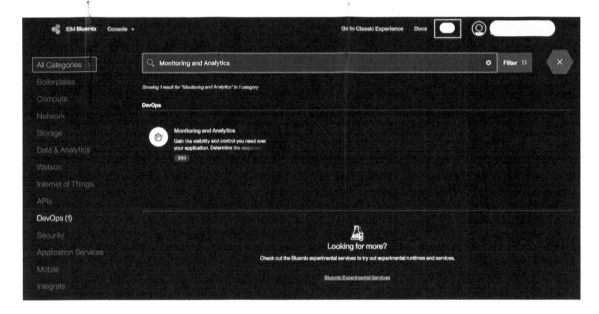

2. Click **Monitoring and Analytics** service. The service details are displayed as shown here:

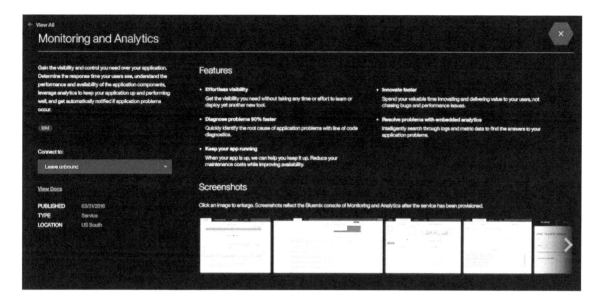

3. The available plan details of the M&A service are as shown in the following screenshot. Enhanced monitoring and management capabilities are offered under the **Diagnostics** plan. For demonstration here we will use the **Free** plan:

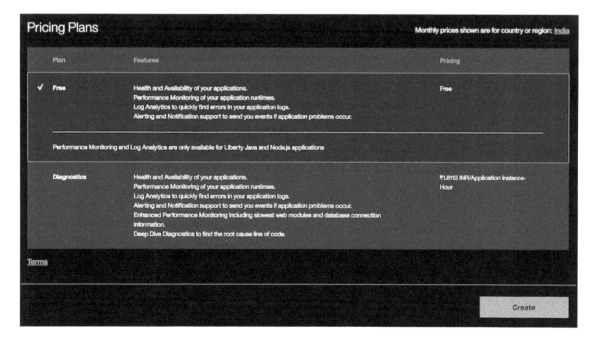

4. Click **Create**. The M&A service is created. You will see that there are no applications bound to the M&A service, hence you will see the message as shown in the following screenshot displayed:

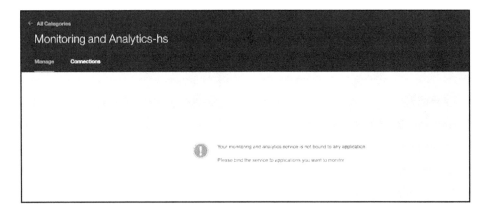

Let us now create a sample application which we can monitor using the M&A service that we just created.

We will use the **JavaCloudantWebStarter** boilerplate to create an application that we will use to demonstrate the monitoring capabilities of the M&A service:

1. From the Bluemix dashboard, go to the **Compute** option. Click on **Get started now!**, as shown in the following screenshot :

2. Select the **Java Cloudant Web Starter** boilerplate:

3. Provide a name for your application. In this demo the application name is `mnademo-b05307`. Leave the other fields with their default values, as shown here:

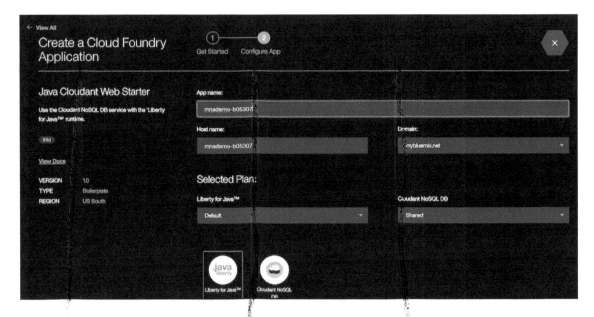

4. Click **Create**. This creates the starter application.

In this section, we will learn how to bind the M&A service you created with your application:

1. Once the application is started, go to the **Connections** view of your application, as shown in the following screenshot:

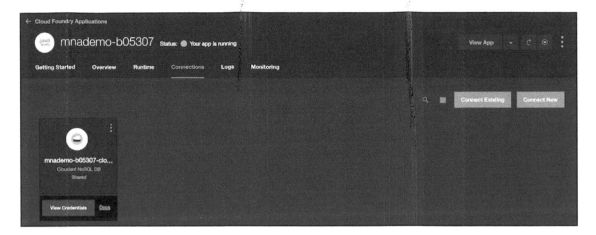

2. To bind the already created M&A service to the application, click **Connect Existing**.

3. Select the M&A service instance that was created earlier. Click **Connect**:

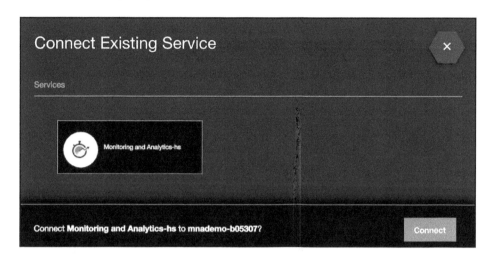

4. You will be prompted to restage the application while binding the service instance to the application. Click **Restage**:

 Binding and restaging of the application will take a few seconds. Please wait patiently for the process to complete.

5. You will now see the M&A service is bound to your application, as shown in the following screenshot:

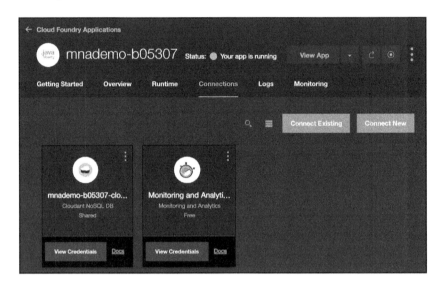

6. Click the M&A service to open the M&A dashboard. Before we look at the various tabs in the M&A dashboard let us make one small configuration under the **Events** tab:

7. Select the gear icon on the top right corner and from the drop-down menu select **Configure events policy**. From the screen displayed, select all the applicable events for which you would like to log events in M&A. Here we will select all the allowed events:

8. Click **Next**. Select all the **Performance** events:

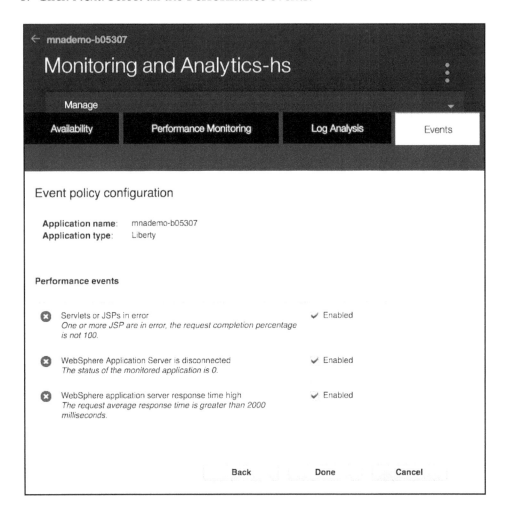

9. Click **Done**.

10. We can also configure e-mail IDs to receive notification e-mails when the configured events occur. For this click again on the gear icon in the **Events** tab and this time select **Configure notification**:

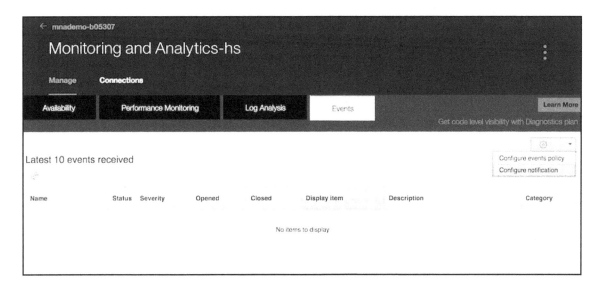

11. Enter the e-mail IDs to which the notification e-mails should be sent when any of configured availability or performance event occur in your application:

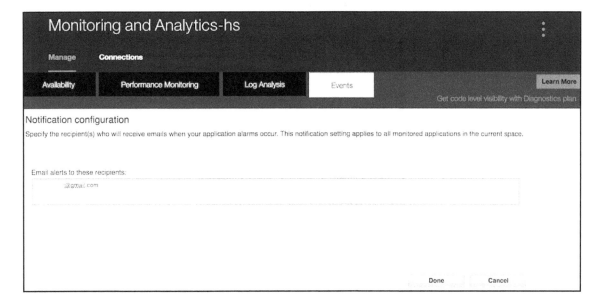

12. Click **Done**.

Simulating events in your application

To simulate events in your application you can do any operations on your application. For this demonstration we will do couple of things:

1. Access the application URL (`https://mnademo-b05307.mybluemix.net/`) and upload a sample file from the application console.
2. Go to the Bluemix dashboard and stop the application:

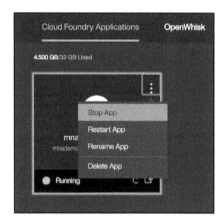

3. Start the application after a minute or so:

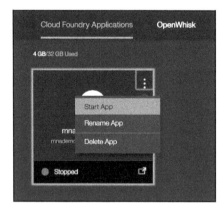

Let us now look at what the M&A service offers as part of monitoring your application. We will look at the M&A dashboard in this section:

1. Go to the M&A dashboard by clicking the **M&A** service from under your application, **Connections** view, as explained earlier.
2. In the **Availability** tab, you will see the application availability stats. Here you will see how many times the application URL was not accessible during a given time range. The time range for which you would like to see the report can be adjusted from the **Viewing** dropdown:

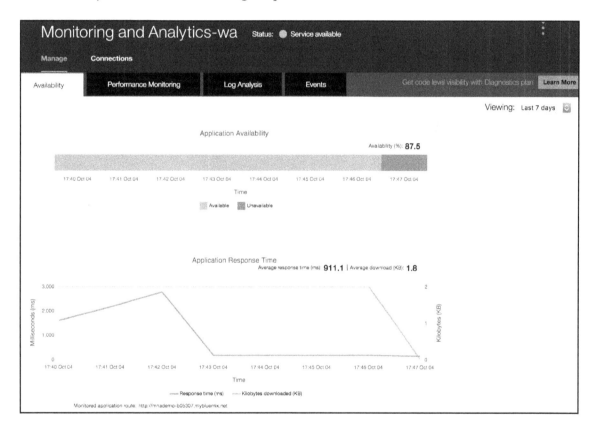

3. You also can see the response time stats for your application requests, as shown in the preceding screenshot.

4. The **Performance Monitoring** tab shows the performance statistics for your application, as the starter application we have bound the service to, is a Java application running on a Liberty server. You will see the JVM usage, Java heap size usage, thread pool count, and garbage collection stats, as shown in the following screenshot:

5. The **Log Analysis** tab enables you to query on the logs for your application:

For details on querying and analyzing the application logs from the **Log Analysis** tab, you can refer to `https://ibm.biz/BdrHvk`.

6. You can filter log events based on the filter strings you can see to the left of the screen in the **Log Analysis** tab.

7. For example, the logs for your application consist of `responseCode 200`, and all occurrences of this can be filtered by selecting `200` under the response code. This adds the filter string to the **Search** field. Click **Search** to see the relevant logs which have logged a response code of `200`. You can add more conditions to build the filter string and filter the logs records you want to view:

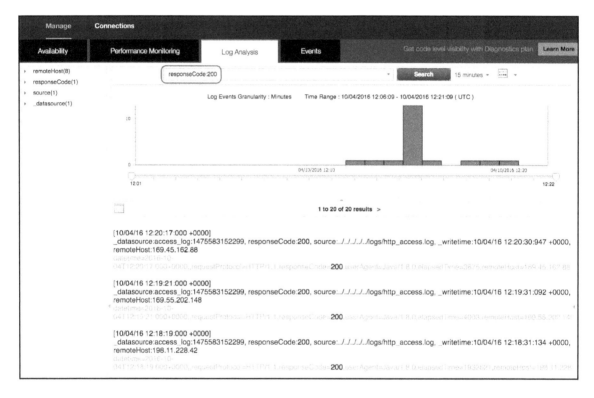

8. In the **Events** tab, you will see an availability event logged. This was logged when we simulated an application downtime by stopping the application in the previous section:

9. Let us verify if the notification e-mail was sent as configured. Go to the inbox for the e-mail ID, which was configured in the step where we configured notification for the events in the M&A service. The following screenshot shows the inbox view for the ID that was configured in this demonstration. You will see there are two e-mails received:

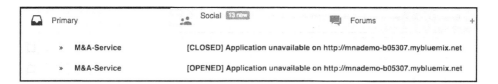

10. The first e-mail was received when the application URL was not available. This happened when we stopped the application. E-mail contents for the availability event is as shown in the following screenshot:

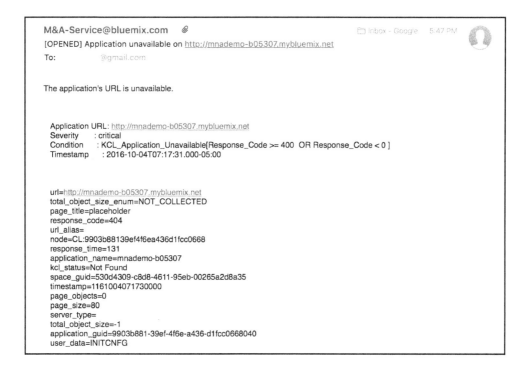

11. The second e-mail was received when the application URL was available again after being unavailable. This happened when we started the application after stopping it. E-mail contents for this event is as shown in the following screenshot:

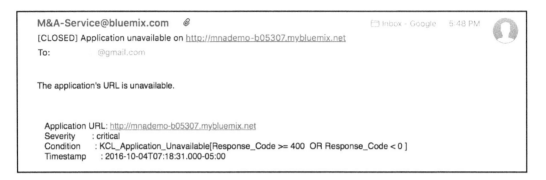

So we have learnt how to create, configure, and use the M&A service to monitor your application across availability and performance. We also looked at the events monitored by the service. If you choose the **Diagnostics plan** feature for the M&A service, you will be able to monitor your application to the code level.

 For additional details on the **Diagnostics plan** feature, you can refer to `https://ibm.biz/BdrHvt`.

New Relic service

The New Relic service is a third-party service which can be used to monitor applications on Bluemix. A user account in New Relic can be created by creating the New Relic instance from Bluemix.

Creating the New Relic service instance

To create the New Relic instance go to the Bluemix catalog using steps that we have carried out earlier while creating the Monitoring and Analytics service. Follow the steps to create the service instance:

1. Filter the services in the catalog by entering **New Relic** in the search field. Click **New Relic** service:

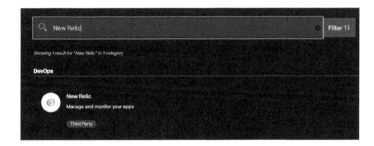

2. **New Relic** is offered under a **Free** plan. Click **Create**:

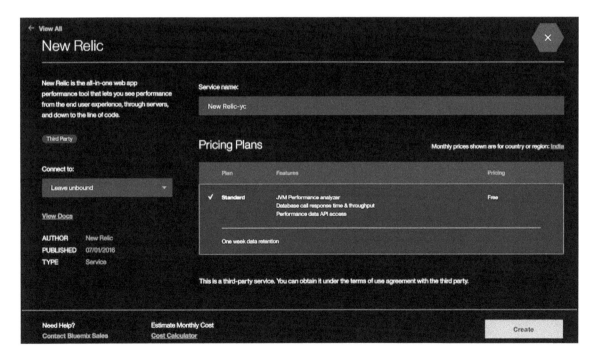

3. Once the service is created, go to the New Relic dashboard by clicking **OPEN NEW RELIC DASHBOARD**:

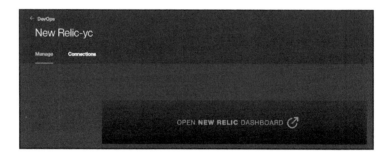

4. This will take you to the New Relic site. You will see a user space created for you. Click on the highlighted area, as shown in the following screenshot:

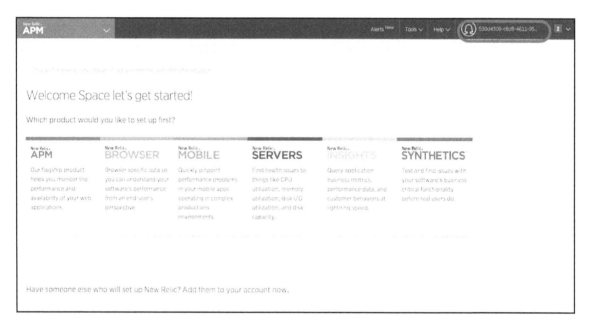

5. Select **Account Settings** from the drop-down menu:

6. The New Relic account details are shown for the user space created. You will see the New Relic license information to the right of this screen. Make a note of this as it will be required in the configuration of our application so that it can send events to New Relic:

This completes the steps where we create the New Relic service instance to monitor our application.

Binding the New Relic service to your application

In this section, we will carry out the steps to bind an application that we want to monitor to the New Relic service instance we created. We will not be creating a new application for this; we will continue to use the same application that we had created to demonstrate the monitoring using the Monitoring and Analytics service:

1. From the application details page, go to the **Connections** view and select **Connect Existing**:

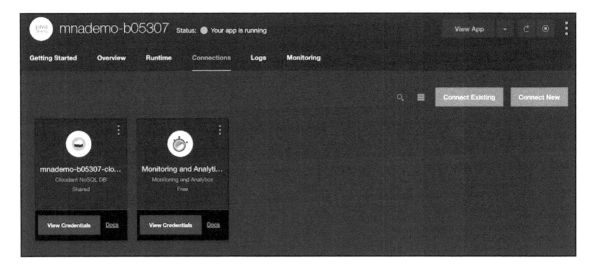

2. Select the **New Relic** service instance that we created. Click **Connect**:

3. Restage the application when you are prompted, by clicking **Restage**.
4. You will see now the New Relic service is bound to the application that you want to monitor using the New Relic service:

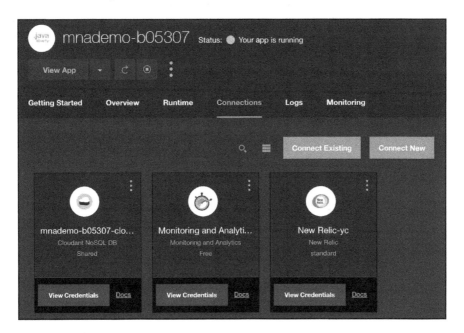

Configuring the application to send events to the New Relic service

To be able to use the New Relic service to monitor your application, you will need to do some configuration at the application deployment end, which is discussed in this section:

1. Go to the application **Overview**. Click the **Add Git Repo and Pipeline** option, as shown in the following screenshot:

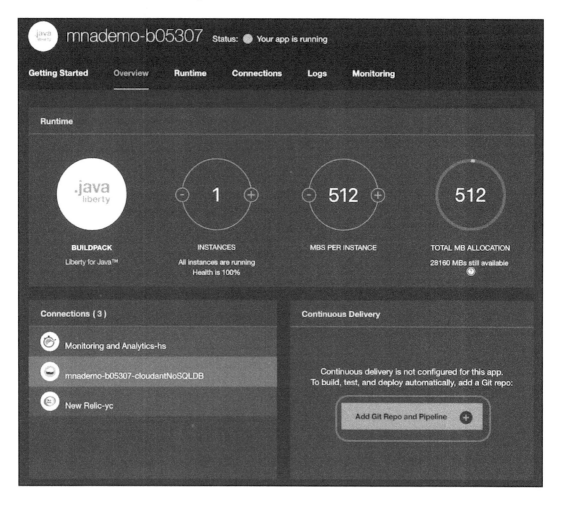

This will create a project for your application in the Git repository. If you are not already logged into IBM DevOps you will be prompted to log in. Use the same credentials as your IBM ID, which you have used while logging in to Bluemix.

Before proceeding with the repository creation you will be shown a prompt as shown. Ensure that the checkbox against **Populate the repo with the starter app package and enable the Build & Deploy pipeline** is checked:

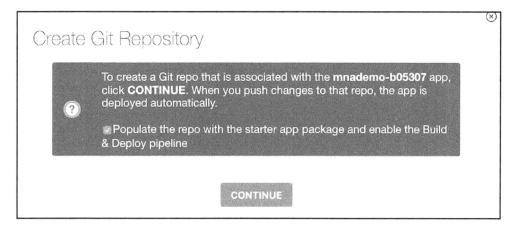

2. Click **CONTINUE**.
3. Once the repository is successfully created for your application, you will get a confirmation as shown here:

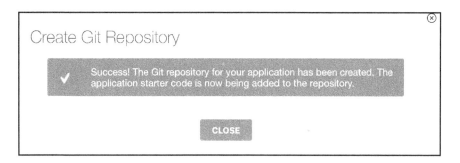

4. Going back to the application **Overview**, you will now see the **GIT URL** link for your repository. Click **EDIT CODE**. This opens the Bluemix DevOps console:

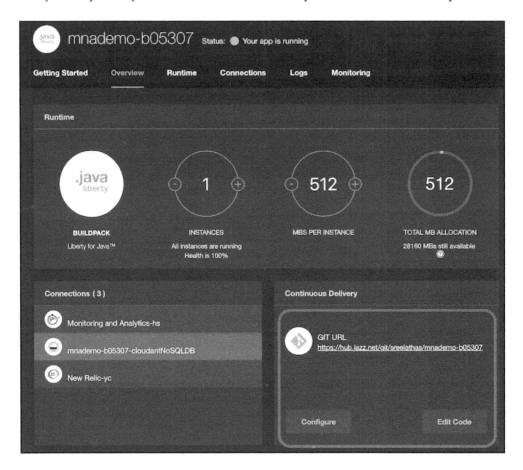

5. Click **BUILD & DEPLOY**. This will take you to the pipeline configured automatically for your application when you had clicked the option to **Add Repo and Pipeline**:

6. You will see two stages in the pipeline. One is **Build Stage** and the other is **Deploy Stage**:

7. Click on the gear icon in **Deploy Stage**. Select **Configure Stage**:

8. The following screenshot shows the existing configuration of the stage:

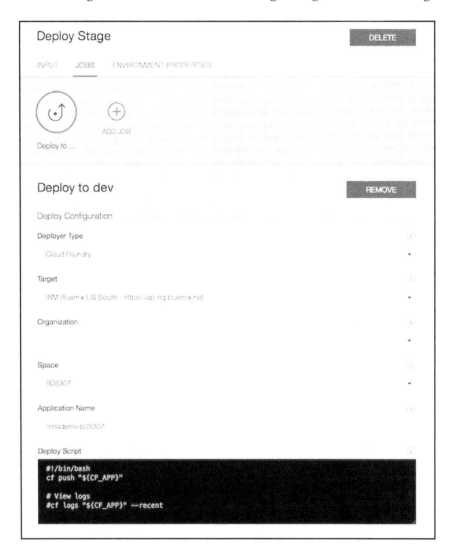

9. You will need to modify the **Deploy Script** terminal, to contain the following
   script:

```
#!/bin/bash
cf push "${CF_APP}" --no-start
cf set-env "${CF_APP}" NEW_RELIC_LICENSE_KEY
  "${NEW_RELIC_LICENSE_KEY}"
cf set-env "${CF_APP}" NEW_RELIC_APP_NAME "${CF_APP}"
```

```
cf start "${CF_APP}"
# View logs
#cf logs "${CF_APP}" -recent
```

10. Click **Save** after making the preceding change to **Deploy Script** in **Deploy Stage**.

11. You will notice that we have added two new lines to the **Deploy Script** terminal. These are used to set the environment variables for the application. We will now need to define these two environment variables with their values.

12. Go to your application details page, select the **Runtime** view. Go to the **Environment Variables** tab:

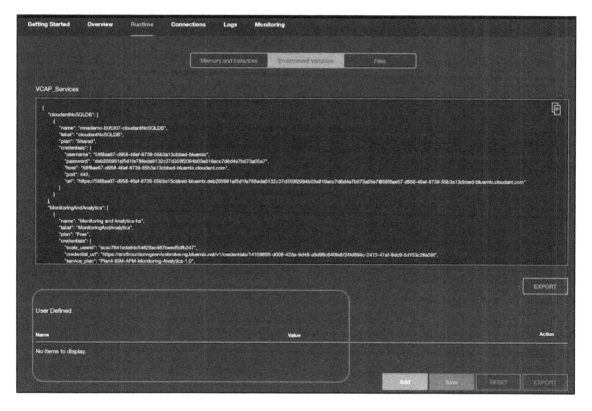

13. We will define the two variables under the **User Defined** properties. Click **Add**. Add the following two name value pairs and click **Save**:

```
NEW_RELIC_LICENSE_KEY=<value got from New Relic site>
NEW_RELIC_APP_NAME=<value of app name used in the deploy script,
    mnademo_b05307 in case of this example>
```

The following screenshot shows the properties set for this demonstration:

14. Now go back to the IBM DevOps console and go to the pipeline for your application. Click the play icon to run **Build Stage**. Once the build completes, click the play icon to run **Deploy Stage**:

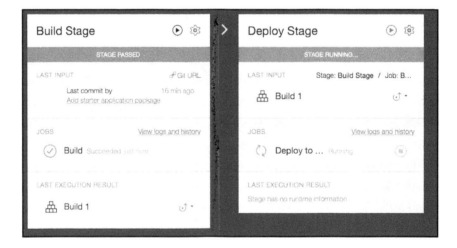

15. Once **Deploy Stage** completes successfully, you are ready with your application to be monitored by New Relic:

Before we can look at New Relic reports, let us simulate some activities within the application.

Simulating events in your application

We will simulate activity in the application by going to the application URL (`https://mnademo-b05307.mybluemix.net`) and performing some operations using the application console, such as uploading the file and so on.

Viewing reports in the New Relic dashboard for your monitored application

We shall now go to the New Relic dashboard to view the monitoring reports from New Relic for your application:

1. Go to the New Relic dashboard, as described earlier. In the dashboard, select **APM**. Here you will see your application listed, as shown in the following screenshot:

2. Click the application to view the monitoring reports for your application, as shown here:

3. You can also look at reports from JVM monitoring for your application in addition to the other reports and stats that you can view based on the options available from the left of the screen:

Summary

In this chapter, we learnt about the different services that can be used to monitor and manage your applications. We learnt to work with the Monitoring and Analytics service for a web application deployed on Bluemix. Additionally, we also learnt to work with New Relic which is a third-party service on Bluemix.

You can also explore the **Availability Monitoring** service from the Bluemix services catalog, to monitor the response time and uptime of your application.

In the next chapter, we will learn about the different compute options available in Bluemix and when to use them. We will also learn to develop and deploy applications on some of the available compute options.

7
Compute Options on Bluemix

Compute capability provides Bluemix users with infrastructure resources with which they can deploy and run their applications. There are different flavors of compute supported on Bluemix. At the time of writing, the different compute options available are:

- Cloud Foundry applications (also referred to as instant runtimes)
- Containers (based on Docker)
- Virtual servers (based on Open Stack APIs)
- OpenWhisk (for event-based applications)

 At the time of writing, OpenWhisk is offered as experimental.

When you log in to Bluemix, and select the **Compute** option, you will see the different compute options available on Bluemix, as shown in the following screenshot:

In this chapter, we will learn more about these compute options. Let's start with Cloud Foundry applications.

Cloud Foundry applications

As explained in earlier chapters, Bluemix is a Cloud Foundry-based platform as a service offering, which means that its application infrastructure and automation is enabled by the Cloud Foundry project.

In earlier chapters, we have seen how to work with Cloud Foundry-based applications on Bluemix, we have also seen how we can work with cf cli or Bluemix UI to create Cloud Foundry-based apps and deploy them on Bluemix. In this chapter, we will look at yet another way to work with Cloud Foundry-based applications.

Working with the eclipse plugin for Bluemix

In this section, we will learn to use eclipse IDE for the development of apps and see how the Bluemix plugin for eclipse facilitates for a seamless and easy integration with your public Bluemix account.

Installing the eclipse plugin for Bluemix

The minimum version of eclipse required for the plugin is eclipse Luna (4.4.1) and above.

> Refer to the plugin details at
> `https://marketplace.eclipse.org/content/ibm-eclipse-tools-bluemix`.

Perform the following steps for plugin installation:

1. Having installed the supported version of Eclipse, open the Eclipse editor.
2. Go to **Help** | **Eclipse Marketplace**.
3. Enter `Bluemix` in the **Find** field and click on **Go**.
4. You will see the available plugins, as shown in the following screenshot.
5. Click **Install** on the plugin highlighted in the following screenshot:

6. Ensure the default options are left selected, as shown in the following screenshot:

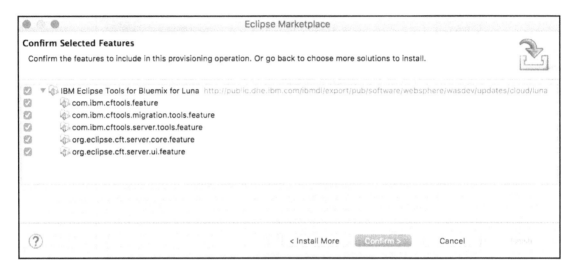

7. Review the license terms and select **I accept the terms of the license agreements**.
8. Click **Finish** to start the plugin installation.
9. Once the plugin installation is completed, you will be shown a prompt to restart Eclipse to complete the installation; select **Yes** to restart Eclipse.

Now let us configure Bluemix as a server that you can use directly from your Eclipse, which is made possible by the plugin that you have just installed:

1. In Eclipse, open **Servers View**.

See **Eclipse Help** for details on opening views in Eclipse.

2. To create a new server, right-click in **Servers View** and select **New** | **Server**.

3. For the server type, expand **IBM** and select **IBM Bluemix** in the server creation wizard, as shown in the following screenshot:

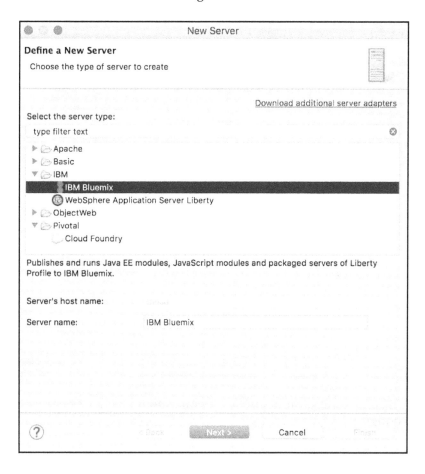

4. You will now be prompted to enter the credentials to connect to your public Bluemix account, as shown in the following screenshot:

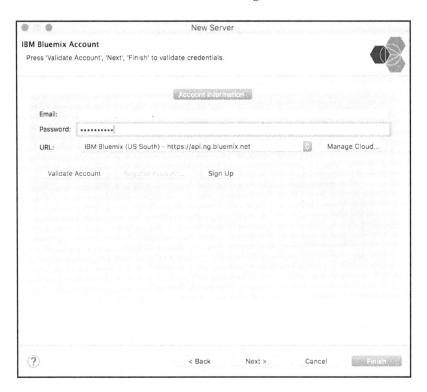

 Creating an account in public Bluemix should be done before you configure a new server in Eclipse, of the server type IBM Bluemix.

5. Click **Validate Account** to connect to your Bluemix account using the credentials and information you have provided. Once the account is validated, you will see a list of your spaces and organizations in Bluemix, as shown in the following screenshot. You can select the space you want to configure Eclipse to work with:

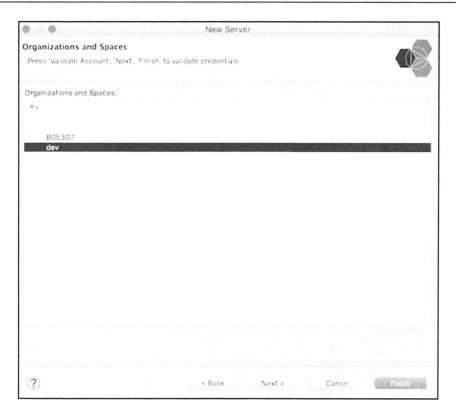

You will now see a new server configuration created, which you can use to deploy and manage Cloud Foundry-based apps that you develop on your Eclipse editor locally:

Now let us look at an example application development experience from Eclipse and use the Eclipse plugin to update the application on Bluemix. I will first create a Cloud Foundry app from the Bluemix dashboard as explained in earlier chapters. I will then download this app and show you an example update to the application and its redeployment to Bluemix, using the Bluemix Eclipse plugin:

If you already have a Java application in Eclipse, then you can use it to deploy on Bluemix, using the plugin you have installed.

1. Create the Cloud Foundry app from the Bluemix dashboard, using **Java Cloudant Web Starter**, which is a boilerplate:

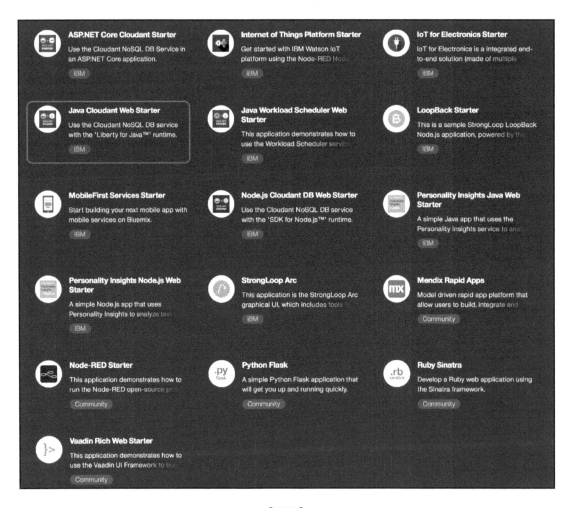

2. Once the app is created, go to the **Getting Started** page, as shown in the following screenshot:

3. Click **Download Starter Code,** as shown in the following screenshot:

The application used in this demo is downloaded as `B05307-07-01-eclipse.zip`, you will get the application archive named based on the name of the application you provide at the time of creating it in Bluemix.

Importing your Cloud Foundry application to Eclipse

 If you are using your own application and not the application from Bluemix, then you can skip the steps in this section.

In order to import the Cloud Foundry application, you have to follow these steps:

1. Go to Eclipse and click **File** | **Import**.

2. From the **Import** wizard, select the option**General | Existing Projects into Workspace**, as follows:

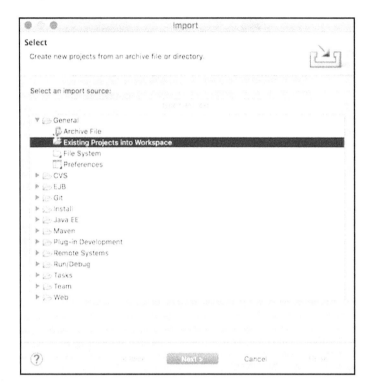

3. Click **Next**.
4. In the subsequent screen, select the option **Select archive file**.

5. Click **Browse** to provide the path of the downloaded app archive location, which is the path to B05307-07-01-eclipse.zip in this example:

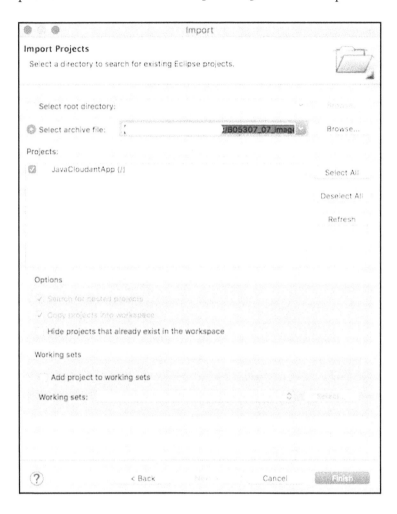

6. Click **Finish** to complete the import of the application files to Eclipse.

In your Java or JEE perspective of Eclipse, you will now see the new project, `JavaCloudantApp`, **created as follows:**

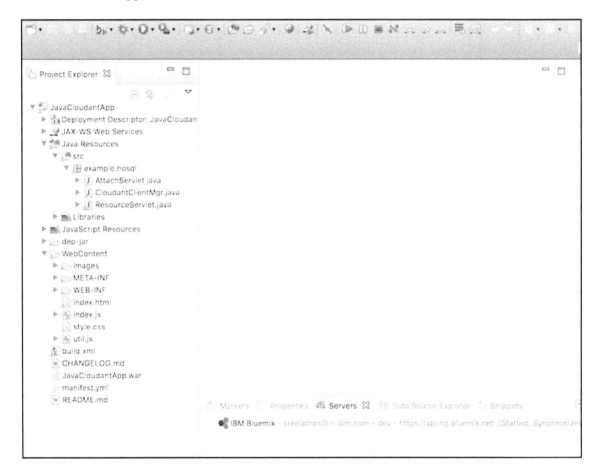

This is a sample Java web application that uses Cloudant NoSQL database as its backend. The Cloudant NoSQL database configured in this application is a service on Bluemix. You will see the service instance created in your Bluemix dashboard, when you created the application.

If you are using your own application, then some of the things that would be different from the example used here would be the services or supporting software, such as the databases that your application is designed to use. If your application uses such vendor provided supporting software, then it is recommended that you figure out whether they are supported as a service on Bluemix. If not, then you will need to program your application with their equivalents, before you can use Eclipse to push your local application to deploy on Bluemix.

You will also see a `manifest.yml` file, which is the one used by Cloud Foundry during deployment.

If you are using your own local application on Eclipse, then you will not have this file. You can choose to create one in the format shown for this sample application.

The content of the `manifest.yml` file for this application is as follows:

If you intend to use any other services on Bluemix while updating or modifying your application in Eclipse, make sure that you update the services section in your `manifest.yml` file to add the names of your services that the application uses.

These services with the given service names should exist in the Bluemix space where you are deploying your application.

Updating your application in Eclipse

You can modify the application to your liking based on what you would want the application to do. For explaining the process, we will make a minor update to the application UI and carry out a local build, and then we shall redeploy the application to Bluemix, using the plugin so that the update is available on your hosted application.

If you go to the existing application route, which is `http://b05307-07-01-eclipse.mybluemix.net/` in the case of this sample demo, you will see the following UI:

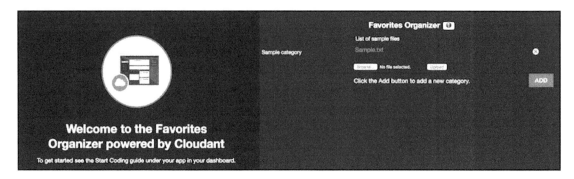

Now let us make a UI update to change the image on the **ADD** button. We will also change the hover text on that button, which is currently showing **Add record**, to **Add file category**:

1. Choose an image file that you want to use instead of the **ADD** button.
2. Copy that image file to the `images` folder in Eclipse, as shown in the next screenshot. The `add_file.png` file is my new image file in this example.
3. Open `index.html` and make the edits, as shown in the following screenshot:

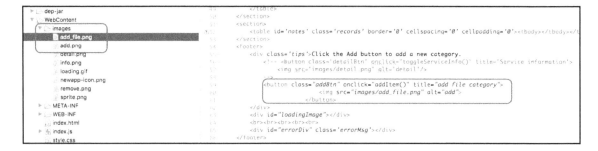

Now we need to run the build locally for the changes to be built into the deployable archive, which is `JavaCloudantApp.war` in this case. You can delete the existing file before building the app with changes, so that you will know that your changes are built when this file is recreated:

1. Delete the existing `JavaCloudantApp.war` archive, highlighted in the following screenshot:

2. Right-click on **build.xml**, and select **Run As | Ant Build** to build the application with your changes:

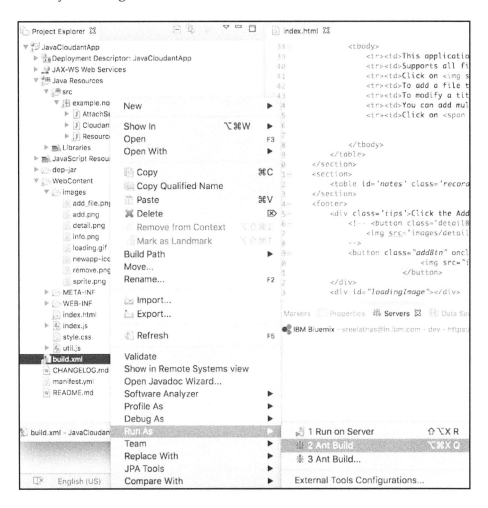

3. Once the build is completed, you will see the `JavaCloudantApp.war` archive created, as shown in the following screenshot:

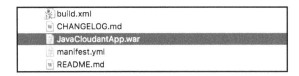

Deploying updates to Bluemix using the Eclipse plugin

The deployment of updates involves the following steps:

1. Right-click on the project in eclipse and click **Run As** | **Run on Server**:

2. In the wizard dialog, you can choose the existing server configuration, which was created earlier in this chapter for **dev** space in your Bluemix account.

If you want to deploy the application in any other space on Bluemix, or another organization or region, you can do so by choosing the **Manually define a new server** option. You need to ensure that the Bluemix services, your application is dependent on, are configured in the space you are planning to deploy in.

3. We will choose the existing server, as we are updating the application that already exists in the Bluemix space. This is the Space on Bluemix where the configured server will deploy your application, using the Bluemix Eclipse plugin:

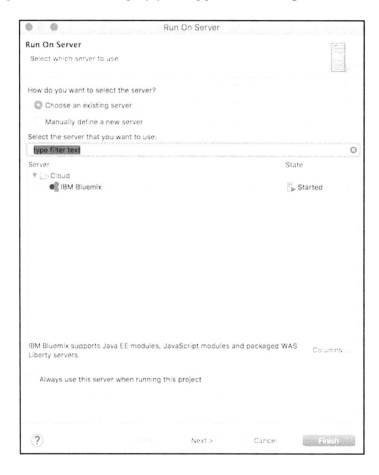

4. Click **Next** and your application will be selected to be configured on the server, as shown in the following screenshot:

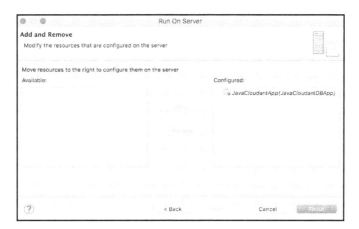

5. Click **Finish**. This will open the application details dialog, which allows you to define how you would like your application to be deployed on Bluemix.

6. You can provide a new name to the application here and have it saved to your `manifest.yml` file locally. In this case, since we are only updating an existing application, we will leave the default values for the **Name** field:

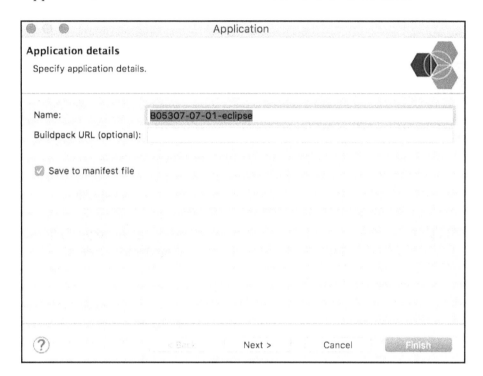

 If you are using any other web server runtime for your application, then you can provide the buildpack URL for it in the **Buildpack URL** field. Details on how to find a buildpack URL for your programming language or framework runtimes was explained in earlier chapters.

7. Click **Next**. Deployment details can be changed in the subsequent dialog. However, for this example, we shall retain the defaults for this application deployment:

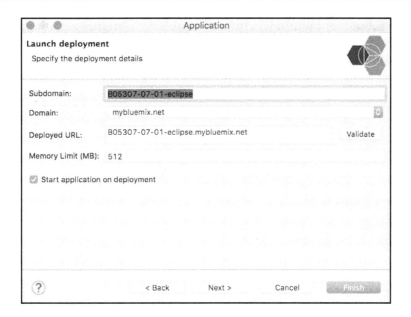

If you want to use another URL for your updated application, you can modify it in the **Deployed URL** field and click **Validate** to check whether it is an available or valid URL to map to your deployed application.

8. Click **Next**.

9. In the subsequent window, you will be able to configure additional Bluemix services that are available in the Bluemix space that you are deploying your application to. By default, the service that is specified in your `manifest.yml` file is pre-selected, as shown in the following screenshot:

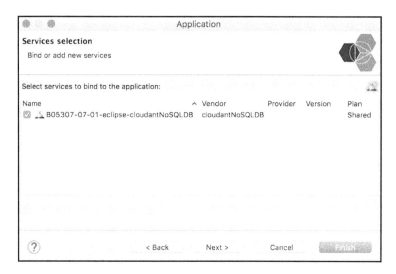

10. Click **Next**.

11. If your application uses any environment variables, you can define them in the subsequent dialog. For this example, we do not have any environment variables to define:

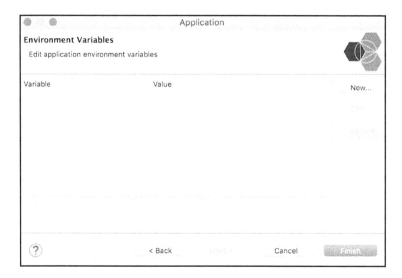

12. Click **Finish** to start the deployment process. You can see the deployment logs in the Eclipse console, as shown in the following screenshot:

When the updated application URL is launched directly from the Bluemix dashboard or in the Eclipse web browser, you will see your updates to the application reflected as follows:

So you have now learned how to work with Eclipse as your local IDE and use your Bluemix account to deploy or host your applications, using the Eclipse Bluemix plugin.

Containers

You can run Docker containers on Bluemix by using the **Containers compute** option. Containers are a great option when you require resource isolation and the portability of your applications and application runtime environments. IBM Containers are based upon Docker container technology. With containers, you have the ability to move dockerized or containerized application environments quickly from development to test, pre-production or production. Additionally, with containers, you can also build highly available applications by using what is called container groups, which are clustered containers, having the same application environment or built from same container image. You can also enable auto recovery while creating a container group; by doing so, new container instances are automatically created if and when any of the already existing containers in the container group go down. A container group can be created even with a single instance of container.

 To get a detailed understanding of how IBM Containers leverage Docker technology, you can refer to `https://ibm.biz/Bdrd67`.

If you are already a Docker user, you can bring your Docker images from Docker Hub to a private registry hosted by IBM and you will be able to use the same images to create containers on Bluemix that are same as the Docker containers you have worked on.

 To know how to go about copying your images from Docker Hub to the IBM registry, you can refer to `https://ibm.biz/BdrdUX`.

Creating an IBM Container with an existing image

In this section, we will learn how to create an IBM Container instance from IBM-provided images. To get the Liberty server in a container, we will build a container from an existing image.

Before you begin

There are a few utilities that are required to be installed locally on your machine, so that you can work with IBM Containers on Bluemix. Make sure you have the following supported versions of utilities installed:

- Docker version 1.6, 1.7, 1.8, 1.8.1, 1.9.0, 1.9.1, or 1.10.0
- Cloud Foundry CLI version 6.14.0 to 6.16.0
- IBM Containers Cloud Foundry plug in

Installing Docker

Based on the operating system you are using, you will need to follow the instructions from the links shown here:

- **OS X**: Get the Docker Toolbox at `https://github.com/docker/toolbox/releases/download/v1.1./DockerToolbox-1.1..pkg`
  - Docker is installed along with Docker Toolbox
- **Windows**: Get the Docker Toolbox at `https://github.com/docker/toolbox/releases/download/v1.1./DockerToolbox-1.1..exe`
  - Docker is installed along with Docker Toolbox
- **Linux**: Refer to the documentation at `https://docs.docker.com/engine/installation/`

The screenshots shown in this section will correspond to Docker installation steps on OS X:

1. Click on the link in the preceding table, corresponding to the OS you are using; here we will use the OS X related link to explain the steps. This will download `DockerToolbox-1.10.0.pkg` to your local system.

2. Double-click on the `.pkg` file to start the installation of the Docker Toolbox.

3. Follow the steps in the wizard to continue with the installation. The components installed as part of the Docker Toolbox installation are shown in the following screenshot:

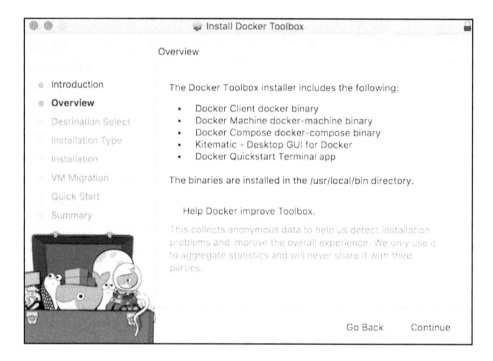

4. Once the installation is complete, you can start working with the Docker terminal. This completes the installation of Docker:

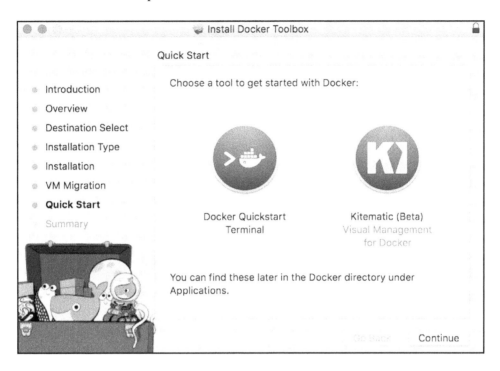

Installing Cloud Foundry CLI

The installation of Cloud Foundry CLI has been explained in an earlier chapter; if you are reading this chapter after carrying out the exercises and demos from earlier chapters then you should already have cf cli on your system. You can find the version of the cf cli by opening the terminal window or command prompt, based on your OS, and typing the following command:

```
cf -v
```

The results of running this command would give you the information on the version of CF CLI that you are using, such as what is shown here:

```
‘        ;-MacBook-F              ;$ cf -v
cf version 6.17.0+5d0be0a-2016-04-15
```

Installing the IBM Containers Cloud Foundry plugin

You will need to run the `cf` command from the following table, based on the operating system you are working on:

OS X	`cf install-plugin` `https://static-ice.ng.bluemix.net/ibm-containers-mac`
Windows 64-bit	`cf install-plugin` `https://static-ice.ng.bluemix.net/ibm-containers-windows_x64.exe`
Windows 32-bit	`cf install-plugin` `https://static-ice.ng.bluemix.net/ibm-containers-windows_x86.exe`
Linux 64-bit	`cf install-plugin` `https://static-ice.ng.bluemix.net/ibm-containers-linux_x64`
Linux 32-bit	`cf install-plugin` `https://static-ice.ng.bluemix.net/ibm-containers-linux_x86`

Install **Cloud Foundry command line** (**cf cli**) plugin before you follow the steps in this section to install the IBM Containers plug-in for cf cli.

The installation steps are as follows:

1. Open your command line or terminal window, based on your operating system, and type the command from the preceding table:

    ```
    cf install-plugin
        https://static-ice.ng.bluemix.net/ibm-containers-mac
    ```

    The following screenshot shows the output generated:

```
-MacBook-Pro:~          ;$ cf install-plugin https://static-ice.ng.bluemix.net/ibm-containers-mac

**Attention: Plugins are binaries written by potentially untrusted authors. Install and use plugins at your own risk.**

Do you want to install the plugin https://static-ice.ng.bluemix.net/ibm-containers-mac? (y or n)> y

Attempting to download binary file from internet address...
12232608 bytes downloaded...
Installing plugin /var/folders/81/g_8p5x257c3bjjsbmfmymyf80000gq/T/ibm-containers-mac...
OK
Plugin IBM-Containers v0.8.897 successfully installed.
```

2. The IBM Containers plugin for Cloud Foundry command line is installed. Type the following command to verify the installation was successful:

```
cf plugins
```

The results of execution are displayed as shown in the following screenshot. You will see the IBM Containers plugin listed as one of the `cf` plugins installed:

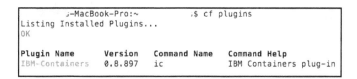

Creating a container using the Bluemix dashboard

We will now learn to create a single container using the Bluemix dashboard.

 You can also create scalable container groups on Bluemix; for detailed steps on how to create them, you can refer to `https://ibm.biz/BdrxyN`.

The following are the steps to create a single container:

1. Log in to your Bluemix dashboard.
2. Click **Compute** from the **Dashboard Categories** and select **Containers**:

3. Click **Get started now!**, shown in the preceding screenshot.

4. This is will display the container images that are available in the private Bluemix registry; we will choose to create a container with WebSphere Liberty installed, so we will choose the **ibmliberty** image, shown in the following screenshot:

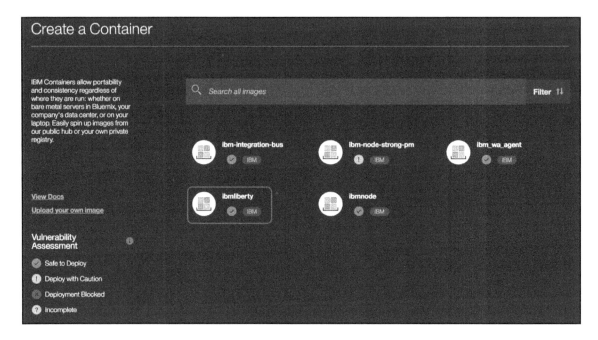

5. Enter the details in the following screen to create your container from the **ibmliberty** image. Enter the container name and choose a size for your container, which defines the memory and storage capacity of the container you are creating. You can also choose to bind a public IP to the container you are creating.

6. Click **CREATE** at the bottom of the screen to start the container creation:

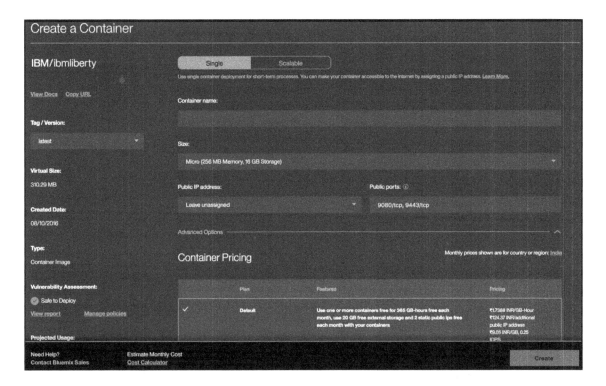

7. Once the container is created, you will see the **Overview** page for the container that you just created, as shown in the following screenshot:

8. If you have not yet requested a public IP, you can do so from the **Overview** page, by clicking the **Request** and **bind a new public IP** option, as shown here:

Once the public IP is bound to your container, you can see it as shown in the screenshot here:

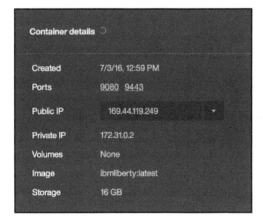

You can also bind Bluemix services to the container you have created. The
Connections tab will show the services that are bound to your container:

You can now see the container you have created in the dashboard view for your **Containers**
compute option, as shown here:

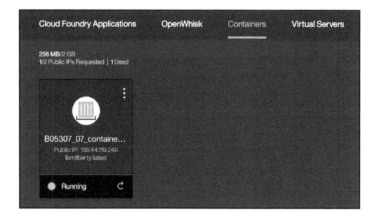

Working with the CF plugin for IBM Containers

Before you can start working with Cloud Foundry IBM Containers plugin, you will need to run the following command from your terminal window or from the command prompt, based on the operating system you are using:

```
cf ic init
```

The results of execution of the command is show here:

```
          -MacBook-Pro:~        $ cf ic init
Deleting the old configuration file...
Generating client certificates for IBM Containers...
Storing client certificates in /Users/s          /.ice/certs/...

Storing client certificates in /Users/          /.ice/certs/containers-api.ng.bluemix.net/9a2ff98e-b9b3-420a-9b45-05c1039fc90b...

OK
The client certificates were retrieved.

Checking local Docker configuration...
You are authenticated with the IBM Containers API,
however, the local Docker daemon is not reachable to authenticate it
with the IBM Containers registry. You can still run IBM Containers
commands, but you cannot push or pull images until you start the local Docker daemon.

You can choose from two ways to use the Docker CLI with IBM Containers:

Option 1: This option allows you to use 'cf ic' for managing containers on IBM Containers while still using the Docker CLI directly to manage your local D
ocker host.
          Use this Cloud Foundry IBM Containers plug-in without affecting the local Docker environment:


          Example Usage:
          cf ic ps
          cf ic images

Option 2: Use the Docker CLI directly. In this shell, override the local Docker environment by setting these variables to connect to IBM Containers. Copy
and paste the following commands:
          Note: Only some Docker commands are supported with this option. Run cf ic help to see which commands are supported.
          export DOCKER_HOST=tcp://containers-api.ng.bluemix.net:8443
          export DOCKER_CERT_PATH=/Users/          /.ice/certs/containers-api.ng.bluemix.net/5a2ff98e-b9b3-420a-9b45-05c1039fc90b
          export DOCKER_TLS_VERIFY=1

          Example Usage:
          docker ps
          docker images
```

To get the details on the container that you just created, so as to work with it using the command line plugin, you will need to execute the following command:

```
cf ic ps
```

This command will list all the containers you have created within your Bluemix organization.

The result of execution of this command is shown in the following screenshot; you will see the single container that we just created is listed along with other details about the container such as its ID, name, and so on:

```
          -MacBook-Pro:~        $ cf ic ps
CONTAINER ID    IMAGE                                       COMMAND    CREATED         STATUS                  PORTS
                                          NAMES
b5983581-66f    registry.ng.bluemix.net/ibmliberty:latest   ""        15 minutes ago  Running 15 minutes ago  169.44.119.249:9080->9080
/tcp, 169.44.119.249:9443->9443/tcp    B05307_07_container_demo
```

For a detailed reference on the cf cli IBM Containers plugin commands, you can refer to `https://ibm.biz/BdrxMD`.

Virtual servers

Virtual servers are a solution to spawn computing resources with specifications that suite your workload. IBM offers compute capability on Bluemix using virtual servers based on Open Stack. Virtual servers give users the flexibility to develop and host applications in an environment that is fully under their control, there are no restrictions in terms of operating system, supporting software, or other resources when using virtual servers.

To learn more about how to create and use virtual servers, you can refer to `https://ibm.biz/BdrxM4`.

From the Bluemix dashboard's **Compute** category, click **Virtual Servers** to go to the screen where you can get started with virtual servers. Click **Get started now!** to start creating the virtual server:

At the time of writing this book, virtual servers on Bluemix are in beta. This beta support for new Bluemix users is closed, hence we will not be able to take you through the steps of creating the virtual server on Bluemix; however, to learn more about virtual servers and for steps to get started with virtual servers, you can refer to the link provided earlier.

OpenWhisk

OpenWhisk is an event-driven compute platform. OpenWhisk allows application developers to write and host application logic agnostic of the infrastructure on which it will run. This application logic is then triggered through events that can come from Bluemix services or other applications or sources. Such application logic are also called as actions. The uniqueness of this compute platform is that it is triggered only when an event occurs, which means that the trigger caused by an event will result in the application on OpenWhisk to be deployed and executed; if no event occurs the application unit does not run and hence does not use any infrastructure resources:

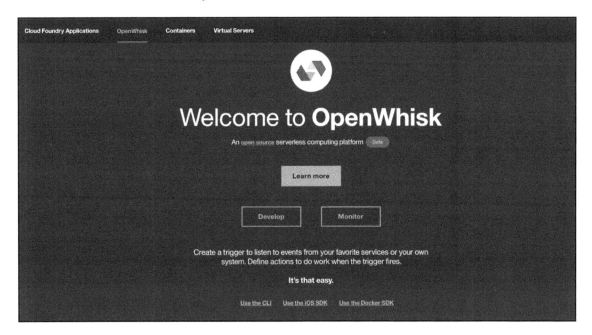

At the time of writing this book, OpenWhisk is in beta. To know the scope for use and support for experimental services, you can refer to `http://ibm.co/2dMu4f7`.

You will see the editor, where you can write the application logic or actions. A sample Hello World action written in JavaScript is provided. You can make changes to the file in the editor and can run the action by clicking **Run This Action**:

The terminology that you will need to understand to work with OpenWhisk are as follows:

- **Actions**: An application logic that runs when an event occurs is called an action.
- **Triggers**: An event that triggers a certain action to occur is called a trigger.
- **Rules**: A rule associates a trigger to an action. A rule defines what action happens when a certain trigger occurs or is fired.
- **Sequence**: An action can be defined in a way such that it is a sequence of multiple actions.

You can work with OpenWhisk using the Bluemix UI, OpenWhisk CLI, or by using an iOS mobile SDK. Here we will look at using the OpenWhisk CLI.

Installing the OpenWhisk CLI

The OpenWhisk tool is also called the wsk command line tool.

You will need to follow the steps at `https://ibm.biz/BdrxMfto` to install wsk command line tool.

 Make sure pip is already installed on your system before you attempt to install the wsk command line tool.

The results of executing the `pip install` command for OpenWhisk on the system used for this demo is as shown in the following screenshot:

```
          -MacBook-Pro:~          ,$ sudo pip install --upgrade https://new-console.ng.bluemix.net/openwhisk/cli/download

Collecting https://new-console.ng.bluemix.net/openwhisk/cli/download
  Downloading https://new-console.ng.bluemix.net/openwhisk/cli/download
    | 71kB 95kB/s
Installing collected packages: openwhisk
  Running setup.py install for openwhisk ... done
Successfully installed openwhisk-0.1.0
```

You will need to copy the commands from the URL mentioned previously and run them in your terminal window or command prompt, based on your operating system, to complete the wsk tool installation and configuration.

Creating the trigger source for our demonstration

Let us learn how to use the Bluemix service as a trigger source. In the example that we used earlier in this chapter, we created a **CloudantNoSQLDB** service instance on Bluemix, we shall now learn how we can configure this Cloudant database as our trigger source. This means that we would like to build a system where we would like some action to happen when there is a change in the Cloudant database we have created earlier:

1. Go to your terminal window and type the following command to get the details of the services you have created within the space you are working on within your organization in Bluemix:

   ```
   cf services
   ```

The result of execution of the command is shown here:

```
           —MacBook-Pro:~              $ cf services
Getting services in org                  / space dev as              ...
OK

name                                    service        plan    bound apps              last operation
B05307-07-01-eclipse-cloudantNoSQLDB    cloudantNoSQLDB  Shared  B05307-07-01-eclipse    create succeeded
```

2. Make a note of the Cloudant service instance name, which is B05307-07-01-eclipse-cloudantNoSQLDB, in this case.

3. Ensure that the OpenWhisk CLI namespace corresponds to your Bluemix organization and space. You can execute the following command to check the namespace from your terminal window:

```
wsk property get --namespace
```

The result of execution of this command gives you the namespace property value that is set in wsk, as shown in the following screenshot:

```
        ;-MacBook-Pro:~              ;$ wsk property get --namespace
whisk namespace          .          ,@in.ibm.com_dev
```

4. If the namespace is not set, you can use the following command to set the property namespace:

```
wsk property set --namespace <Bluemix_Org>_<Bluemix_Space>
```

5. You will need to create a package binding for your Cloudant service instance.

 To know more about Cloudant package you can refer to https://ibm.biz/BdrxMM.

To create the package binding, execute the following command from the terminal window:

```
wsk package refresh
```

This results of this command are shown here:

```
                                    ;$ wsk package refresh
None refreshed successfully!
created bindings:

updated bindings:
Bluemix_B05307-07-01-eclipse-cloudantNoSQLDB_CCS-srv-binding-B05307_07_container_bsrv_demo-1467532601.21
deleted bindings:
```

6. You can create the fully qualified name of the package binding created for your Cloudant data source by executing the following command:

   wsk package list

   The result of execution is as shown in the screenshot here:

```
                                    $ wsk package list
packages
/.                 ).com_dev/Bluemix_B05307-07-01-eclipse-cloudantNoSQLDB_CCS-srv-binding-
B05307_07_container_bsrv_demo-1467532601.21 private binding
```

   Make a note of the package binding name from the results of the execution of the preceding command.

7. To create the trigger, execute the following command:

   ```
   wsk trigger create <name_of_your_cloudanttrigger>
   --feed /<package_binding_name_from_step_above>/changes
   --paramdbname<name_of_cloudant_database_created>
   --paramincludeDoc true
   ```

   The name of the Cloudant database was `sample_nosql_db`, from the example that we created during the Eclipse plugin demonstration. You can use that as `name_of_cloudant_database_created`, in the preceding command. `name_of_your_cloudanttrigger` is the name you would want to give to the trigger you are creating in this demo the name of the trigger created is `B5307_07_CloudantTrigger`, as shown here:

```
                       .$ wsk trigger create B5307_07_CloudantTrigger --feed /.         s@in.ibm.com_dev/Bluemix_B05307-07-01-eclipse-cloudantNo
SQLDB_CCS-srv-binding-B05307_07_container_bsrv_demo-1467532601.21/changes --param dbname sample_nosql_db --param includeDoc true
ok: created trigger feed B5307_07_CloudantTrigger
```

8. You can start polling for changes in your Cloudant database by executing this command:

```
wsk activation poll
```

This will create the listener for any changes in your Cloudant database.

9. Go to the application URL of the application that we created and deployed earlier in this chapter using the Eclipse Bluemix plugin, which is `https://b05307-07-01-eclipse.mybluemix.net/`.

10. Here let us upload a file in the `Sample` category and let us also create a new file category and add another file to this new category, as here:

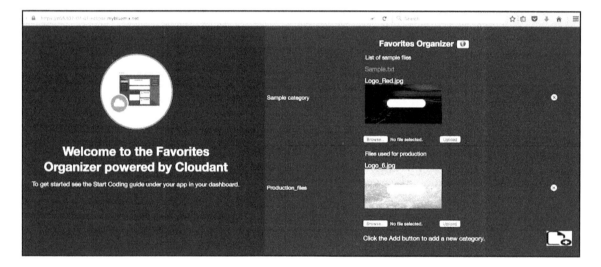

11. Go to your terminal window where you have executed the command for polling the changes to Cloudant database. You will see that the events are created by the trigger when there was a change to the Cloudant database from our actions in the application:

```
                           $ wsk activation poll
Hit Ctrl-C to exit.
Polling for logs
Activation: B5307_07_CloudantTrigger (5692086b52164df7b3e9cc293b9082c7)
Activation: B5307_07_CloudantTrigger (399a77f1cd434654a7cb2c4e1cb2c045)
Activation: B5307_07_CloudantTrigger (79a8c286816f42cf8cec62a2ecc2c031)
Activation: B5307_07_CloudantTrigger (4d5be477dc0246f9b084f0dd52c36578)
```

Creating an action

Let us now look at creating a simple action that can be triggered when the data in the Cloudant database changes. We will see the steps to create an action from the Bluemix dashboard. You can create an action using the wsk command line tool as well:

1. Go to your Bluemix dashboard, and go to **OpenWhisk** under the **Compute** category on your Bluemix dashboard. Click **Develop**, as shown here:

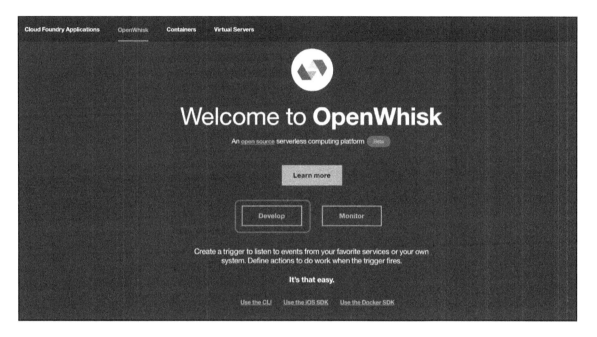

2. The OpenWhisk editor opens, here you can see a **Hello World** action in JavaScript. Click **Create An Action** to create a new action:

3. In the screen shown here, enter the name of your new action. You can choose to code the action in any of the supported programming languages:

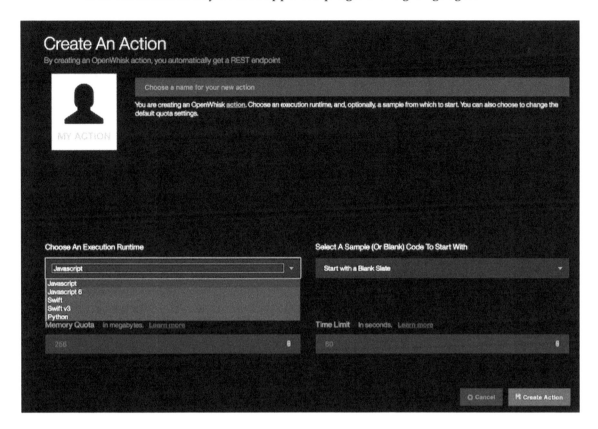

 Since Bluemix is an evolving platform, you may see support for more languages in future.

4. For this example, let us choose **Javascript** as the execution runtime and let us select **Hello World in Javascript** as the sample code, from the second dropdown, as our starting point. Provide a name for your action and click **Create Action**.

5. My new action is now created as shown here, with the starter code; we shall modify the code to print the `_id` value of the Cloudant document that is modified:

```
           MY ACTIONS        Create An Action      Run This Action

 B05307_alert_cloudant_update      B05307_alert_cloudant_update

 Hello World                    /**
                                 *
 Hello World With Params         * main() will be invoked when you Run This Action.
                                 *
                                 * @param Whisk actions accept a single parameter,
                                 *        which must be a JSON object.
                                 *
                                 * In this case, the params variable will look like:
                                 *     { "message": "xxxx" }
                                 *
              MY SEQUENCES       * @return The return value must also be JSON.
                                 *        It will be the output of this action.
 My First Sequence               */
                                function main(params) {
                                    return { "message": "Cloudant database has been updated. _id: " + params._id};
                                }
```

 You can modify the code in your action using the editor in your browser, to build a functionality that you would want to achieve when a certain trigger is fired.

Creating a rule

Rule creates the association or link between the trigger and action. Now that we have created our trigger and our action, let us create a rule to link both, so that when our trigger is fired (in our case caused by Cloudant database update), an action occurs, which is our action created in the previous section, and executes. We will use the `wsk` command line tool to create the rule. Rules can be created from the dashboard as well. Before we create the rule we should make a note of the name of the trigger and the action we would want to link. In our case the trigger is `B5307_07_CloudantTrigger`, and the action is `B05307_alert_cloudant_update`. Lets look at the steps to create a rule:

1. Execute the `wsk` command to create the rule named `B5307-rule`:

```
wsk rule create --enable B05307-rule B5307_07_CloudantTrigger
   B05307_alert_cloudant_update
```

The result of execution is shown in the following screenshot:

```
                              $ wsk rule create --enable B05307-rule B5307_
07_CloudantTrigger B05307_alert_cloudant_update
ok: created rule B05307-rule
ok: rule B05307-rule is active
```

2. The rule is created and can be seen as active in the OpenWhisk editor as well.

Testing a rule

Let us now test to see whether the trigger caused by a Cloudant update leads to the execution of the JavaScript code which you have defined as part of your action:

1. Go to the application URL of the application that we created and deployed earlier in this chapter using the Eclipse Bluemix plugin, which is `https://b05307-07-01-eclipse.mybluemix.net/`, in our demo.

2. Let us delete the existing Sample category and create a new category with the name of `Sample`, and let us upload a simple file to this category, as shown in the following screenshot:

You can make any updates to the Cloudant database that you would like. The preceding changes are for the sake of illustration.

This would have caused your trigger to fire and would have allowed your rule to invoke your action.

3. Go to the OpenWhisk dashboard, **Activity Log** will display the output of the execution of your action code:

You will see that your action was triggered three times due to the updates you performed on your application UI, hence you will see the action code executed three times. You will see that it prints the document `_id` value of the Cloudant document which was updated, as shown here:

Summary

In this chapter, you learned about the different compute options offered on IBM Bluemix. You also learnt about the differences between them and when to use which compute option. You learnt how to work with the Eclipse Bluemix plugin to develop and deploy cloud foundry applications. Further we learnt about creating a single container on Bluemix using an existing image from IBM's private registry. Finally, you learnt about OpenWhisk compute platform for building event-driven applications. This chapter would have given you a good understanding on how to get started with the different compute options on Bluemix. For further examples and how-to(s) you can refer to the links given in each of the sections in this chapter.

In the next chapter, we will learn about the security services available on Bluemix and how to use one of the security services in your application deployed on Bluemix, to provide an authentication service for your application.

8

Security Services on Bluemix

In this chapter, we will look at what security services are available on Bluemix and how we can use them to secure our application on Bluemix. Securing your web applications and your cloud environment is a very important aspect of developing applications on cloud. In this chapter, you will learn about the security services provided on Bluemix and how you can configure one of the security services to provide an authentication service to your web application.

 Discussions in this chapter will be based upon the capabilities that are available on Bluemix at the time of writing this book.

In this chapter, you will learn about the following topics:

- Overview of security services in Bluemix
- Access Trail security service
    - Creating the Access Trail service instance
    - Working with the Access Trail service
- Single Sign On security service
    - Creating the Single Sign On service instance
    - Configuring the identity sources in Single Sign On
    - Configuring the Cloud Directory
    - Configuring LinkedIn as an identity source
    - Configuring Google+ as an identity source
    - Creating an application that will use the Single Sign On service as an authentication service

- Modifying the sample application to enable the use of the Single Sign On service
- Integrating the Single Sign On service with your application

Overview of the security services in the Bluemix catalog

Services under the **Security** category in the Bluemix catalog are as follows:

- **Access Trail**, which is an IBM service, in beta at the time of writing this book
- **Application Security** on Cloud is an IBM-provided service
- **Single Sign On** is an IBM-provided service
- **Adaptive Security Manager** (**ASM**) is a third-party service

When you log in to Bluemix and select the Security category, you will see the security services created in your account:

From here you can create a new security service instance by clicking the **Get started now!** icon in the top-right corner, as shown in following screenshot:

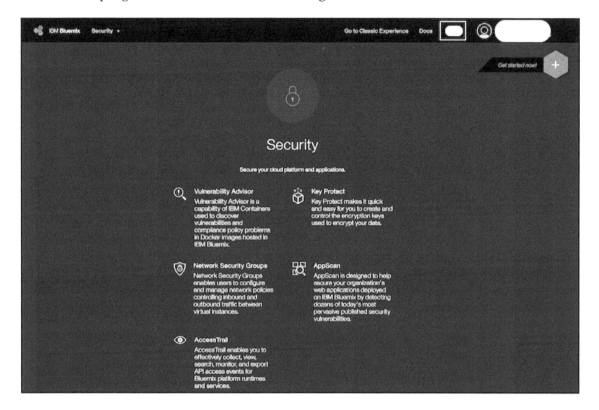

Clicking the **Get started now!** icon, will display the security services available on Bluemix. At the time of writing this book, the available security services are as shown in the following screenshot:

Let us now look at some of these security services, what they offer as security functions, and how they can be used with your application on Bluemix.

Access Trail security service

Access Trail is an IBM service that allows you to monitor security within an IBM Cloud environment.

 This service is in beta at the time of writing this book.

Access Trail uses API call monitoring as the mechanism to monitor the IBM Cloud. When using the Access Trail service, all API calls in the IBM Cloud are monitored and any suspicious or unusual API activity is detected. Remedial measures to prevent the security breaches are carried out by preventing the specific API activity in the IBM Cloud environment. The Access Trail service captures API call logs, which is later used for filtering and monitoring the API call activity in the IBM Cloud. All APIs from IBM Cloud runtimes, services, applications, and user activity are logged.

 You can read the blog at `https://ibm.biz/BdrFDt` for more information on Access Trail.

Creating the Access Trail service instance

In this section, we will learn how to create the Access Trail service instance and how to configure it to monitor your cloud environment, in this case Bluemix:

1. Log in to your Bluemix account.
2. Click **Security** category and from the security services dashboard, click **Get started now!**

3. From the list of security services, select **Access Trail**, as shown in the following screenshot:

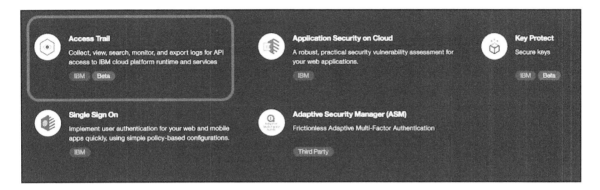

4. Click **Create** after reviewing the information shown on the screen, as shown in the following screenshot:

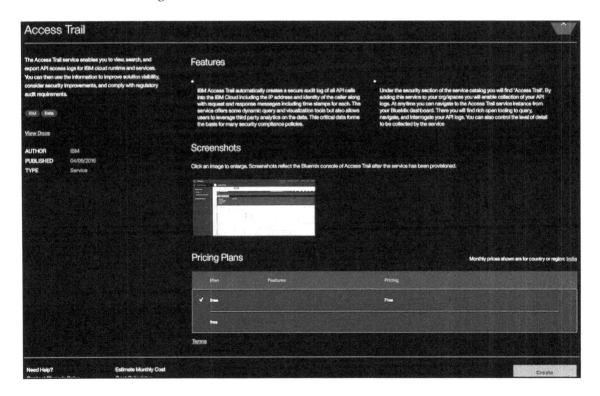

5. Once the service instance is created, you will see the screen, as shown in the following screenshot, for the created service instance. The **Log level** option can be selected to be among the options shown in the dropdown, as shown in the following screenshot:

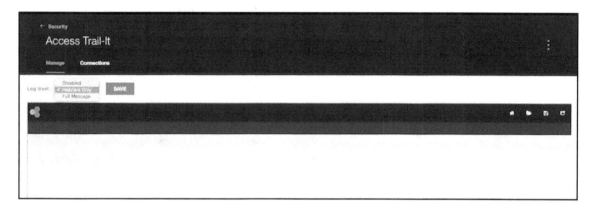

Working with the Access Trail service

You don't have to bind any application to the Access Trail service. You can manage any space in your Bluemix account using the Access Trail service.

We will use the sample application that we developed in Chapter 2, *Building and Deploying Your First Application on IBM Bluemix*, which was developed using the Personality Insights Java Web Starter boilerplate. Assuming that this application (java-pi-hw-01) is on your Bluemix space where the Access Trail service is created, let us launch the application URL and perform a couple of actions on the application. This application makes calls internally to Watson/Alchemy services. Let us look at the API calls logged as part of this activity:

1. Open the Access Trail dashboard. You can configure the dashboard based on how you would like to see the reports. The following screenshot shows such a sample API activity in the Bluemix space used for demonstration:

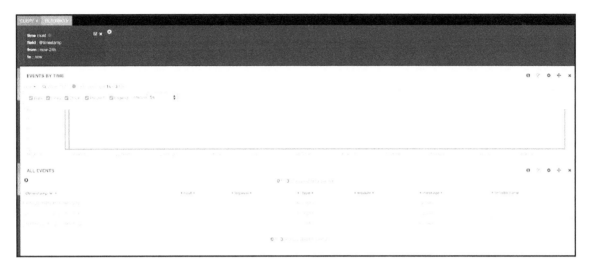

2. You can create queries based on what information you would like to filter out of the recorded API activity logs.

   If you want to create your queries and filters for monitoring the activity log in your Bluemix space, you can refer to `https://ibm.biz/BdrFD7`.

3. Expanding the row in the Access Trail dashboard will give the details of the API calls that resulted from the activity we performed using our application (`java-pi-hw-01`) URL. The details are as shown in the following two screenshots:

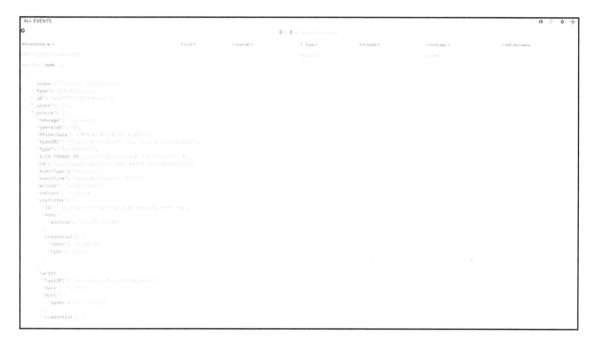

The remaining details are shown in the following screenshot, it is a continuation of the content from the preceding screenshot:

```
'observer':
   "id": "a86ge92-t205-4227-8372-5f7674abd8e87,
   "name": "cnymservice",
   "host": {
      "address": "cloudoqueve.bluemix.net"
   },
   "credential": ,
"requestPath": "/v1/adfcdyhiyhvexh/d/dv77shevcbtd-cd7yuds55.d57387777cst",
"reason":
   "reasonCode": "uone",
   "reasonType": "http"
},
"severity": "normal",
"tags":
,
"attachments": [
   {
      "typeURI": "h:r:cs:cs:txser:v",
      "contentType": "l:v:v:v:v:v:eh:v:v",
      "content": "..."
   },
   {
      "typeURI": "response:header",
      "contentType": "application/json",
      "content": "..."
   }
],
"reporterchain":
   "role": "new",
   "reporterId": "...",
   "reportedTime": "2016-01-01-01-01.01215T"
},
"uori": {
   "name": "infsrnvpoiv:tesrv:nerv",
   "id": "3385-05-4545-4222-5535-757465f5ds",
   "createdAt": "2016-01-01T01:00:292"
}
```

Single Sign On security service

In this section, we will learn about another useful security service on Bluemix, called Single Sign On. We will learn to create the service instance, configure it, and integrate it with your web application on Bluemix.

Creating a Single Sign On service instance

Let's see how to create a Single Sign On service instance:

1. Log in to your Bluemix account.
2. Click the **Security** Category and from the Security Services dashboard, click **Get started now!**:

3. From the list of security services, select **Single Sign On**, as shown in the following screenshot:

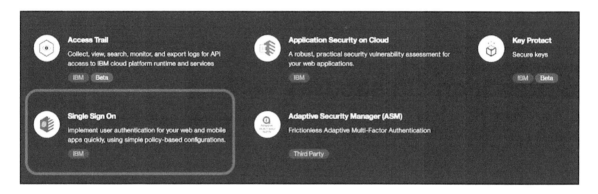

4. Click **Create** after reviewing the information shown on the screen, as shown in the following screenshot:

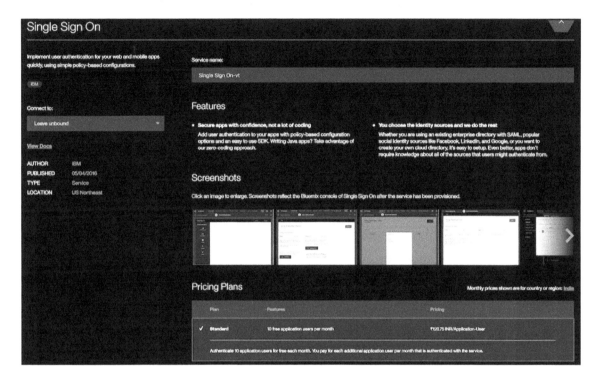

5. Once the service instance is created, you will see the screen shown in the following screenshot, where you will be prompted to enter a name for your service, which will be part of your service URL:

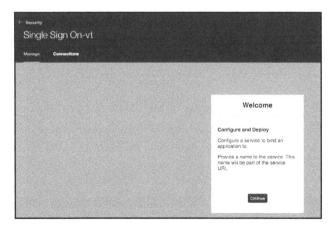

6. Click **Continue**.

7. You will see a screen where you can configure an identity provider that you can use to authenticate users to your application:

Supported identity providers are as follows:

- **SAML Enterprise**, using which one can configure the enterprise identity source using SAML tokens
- **Cloud Directory** is a directory of users created and stored in Cloud, which can be configured as an identity source to authenticate users to your application
- Social login refers to sites such as **LinkedIn**, **Facebook**, **Google+**, and **GitHub**

Configuring the identity sources in Single Sign On

In this section, we will see how to configure some of the supported identity sources in the Single Sign On service.

Configuring the cloud directory

Here we will learn the steps to configure your own cloud directory in Single Sign On:

1. To configure the Single Sign On service, let us create an identity source using the **Cloud Directory** option. Click **Cloud Directory**.

2. As shown in the following screenshot, provide a name for your cloud directory:

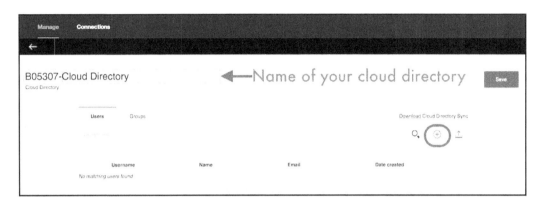

3. Click the + icon to add users to the cloud directory:

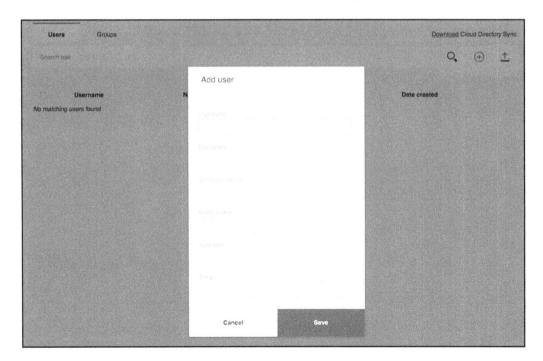

4. Fill out the user details and click **Save** to add users to your cloud directory. Once users have been added, you can choose to group them under specific groups if you wish to. For our demonstration, we will create a couple of users, as shown in the following screenshot:

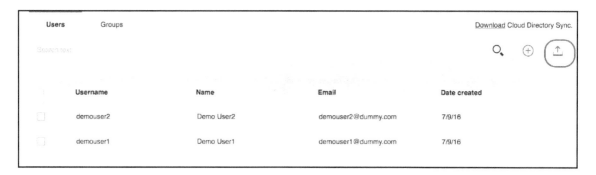

5. You can also do a mass import of users into the cloud directory by using the **User Import** icon. A CSV file with the user details can be imported into the directory from the dialog, as shown in the following screenshot:

6. You can click on the gear icon shown in the following screenshot to configure additional restrictions on user password length and format by selecting a password policy. You can also create client credentials for API access:

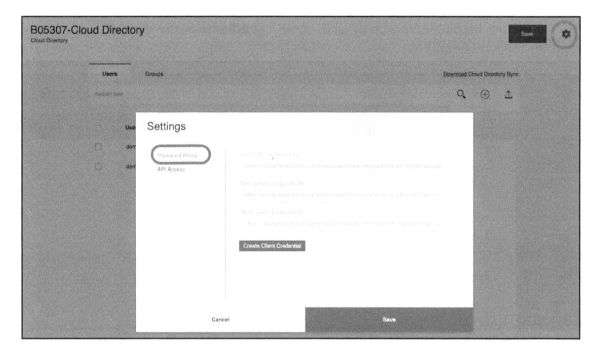

Configuring LinkedIn as an identity source

Here we will learn the steps to configure a social identity source such as LinkedIn in Single Sign On:

1. From the Single Sign On dashboard, select **LinkedIn** as the identity source you want to configure:

2. Provide a name for your LinkedIn identity source. To configure LinkedIn as your identity source, there are two steps that you need to follow, which are shown in the following screenshot:

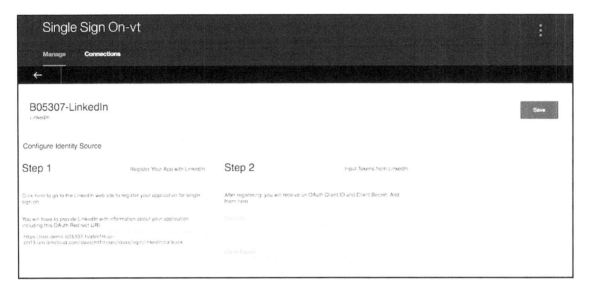

3. Follow the instructions in Step 1, go to the LinkedIn website, and register your application, which would need authenticated access through the user's LinkedIn accounts. Once your application is registered, you will get a **Client ID** and **Client Secret** keys, which are the authentication keys:

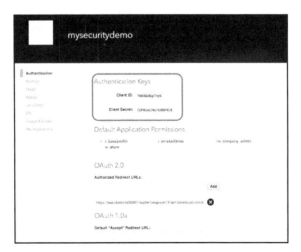

4. Under the OAuth 2.0 of your LinkedIn configuration, you will need to provide the redirect URL. This is the URL that is provided to you under Step 1 in the Single Sign On LinkedIn identity source configuration screen:

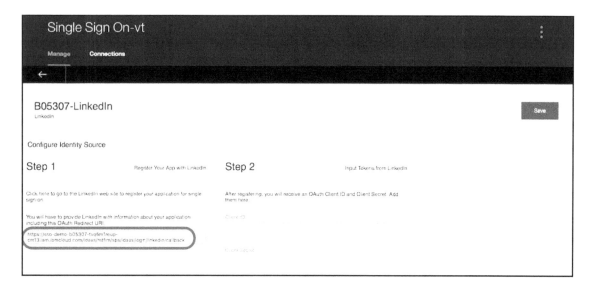

5. Provide this URL as **Authorized Redirect URLs** in the LinkedIn **Authentication** settings for your application and click **Add**:

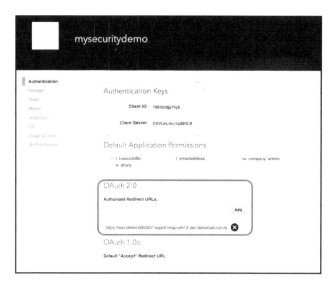

6. Save your application configurations on the LinkedIn website. Go back to the Single Sign On LinkedIn identity source configuration screen. Now we will need to execute Step 2, which is to provide the **Client ID** and **Client Secret** keys we got from LinkedIn by registering our application in earlier steps:

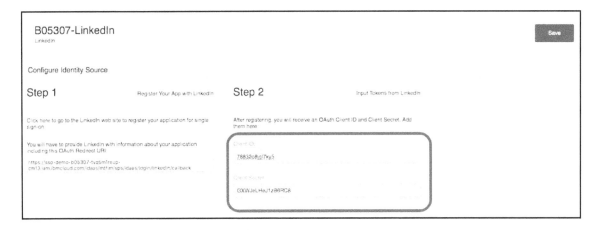

7. Click **Save**. You will see that the LinkedIn identity source is created and enabled:

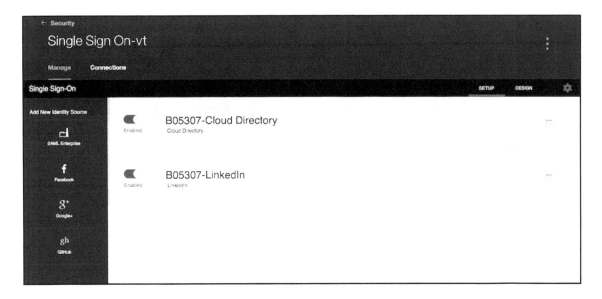

8. Similarly, go ahead and create another identity source using Facebook, using the same set of instructions as followed for LinkedIn. Once you register your application on the Facebook website, you will get an **App ID** and **App Secret**, which need to be provided as part of your identity source configuration in the Single Sign On service, as shown in the following screenshot:

9. Click **Save**. You will see that the Facebook identity source is created and enabled:

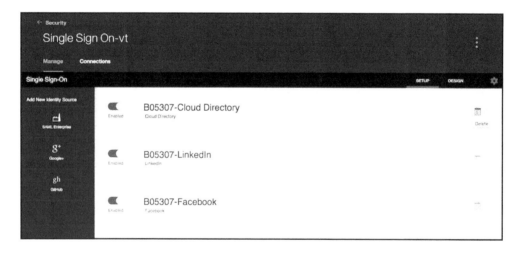

Configuring Google+ as an identity source

Here we will learn the steps to configure Google+ as a social identity source in Single Sign On:

1. From the Single Sign On dashboard, select **Google+** as the identity source you want to configure:

2. Provide a name for your **Google+** identity source, as shown in the following screenshot. To configure **Google+** as your identity source, there are two steps that you need to follow, which are shown in the following screenshot:

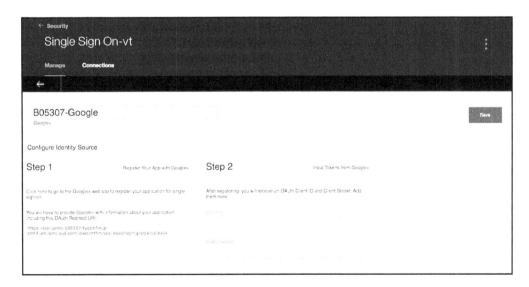

3. Follow the instructions in Step 1, go to the Google+ website, and register your application, which would need authenticated access through the user's Google+ accounts.

4. Once the Google project is created, in the project **Overview**, click **Enable** to enable the Google+ API:

5. Select **Credentials** and click **Create credentials**:

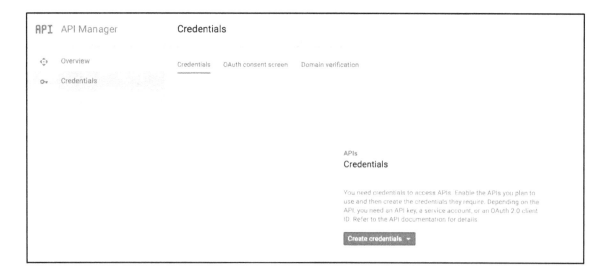

6. Select **OAuth client ID** to configure OAuth credentials:

7. Select the application type as **Web application**. Give a name to the credentials you are creating.

8. Under the authorized redirect URIs, provide the callback URL from Step 2 of the configuration screen for the **Google+** identity source, shown in the Single Sign On service on Bluemix:

9. The OAuth credentials creation screen in Google+ will now be as shown in the following screenshot:

10. Click **Create**. The OAuth credentials are created for your project. You can now copy your client ID and client secret keys:

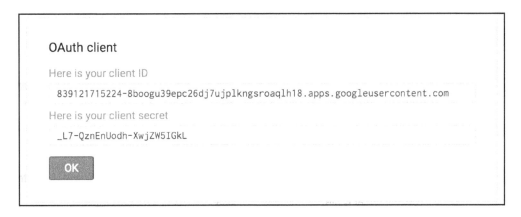

11. The client ID and client secret keys from the preceding step are copied and provided in the configuration screen for Single Sign On using the Google+ identity source. Click **Save**. The Google+ identity source is configured on your Single Sign On service instance:

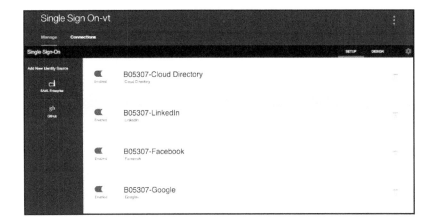

Now you are ready to bind your Single Sign On service to your application on Bluemix and use the authentication services from the configured identity sources for your application.

Create an application which will use the Single Sign On authentication service

To demonstrate the use of the authentication service, let us create a simple Vaadin framework-based application. This also demonstrates the ability to run Vaadin applications on Bluemix:

1. Open your Eclipse IDE. Go to **Help** | **Eclipse Marketplace**.
2. Enter Vaadin in the **Search** field and click **Go**.
3. Vaadin Plugin is returned in the results. Click **Install** to install the Vaadin plugin in Eclipse, so that you can work with Vaadin applications in Eclipse:

4. Once you have the Eclipse Vaadin plugin installed and have restarted Eclipse, let us create a sample Vaadin project, which we will deploy on Bluemix. We will use the out-of-the-box template projects. You can choose to make any changes to the application you want to.

5. In your Eclipse IDE, go to **File | New | Vaadin 7 Project (Maven)**:

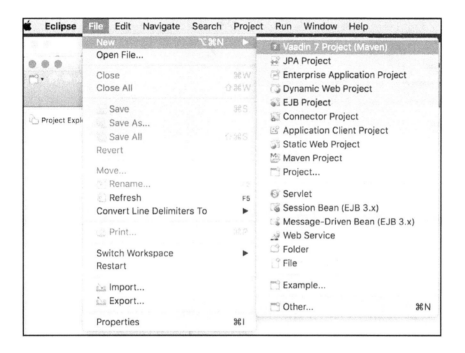

6. You will create the sample CRUD application using the Vaadin framework in Eclipse. Your server view was configured in Chapter 7, *Compute Options on Bluemix*, for IBM Bluemix. In the Eclipse **Server** view, under the IBM Bluemix server runtime, you can see the applications from **dev** space of your Bluemix org, as shown in the following screenshot:

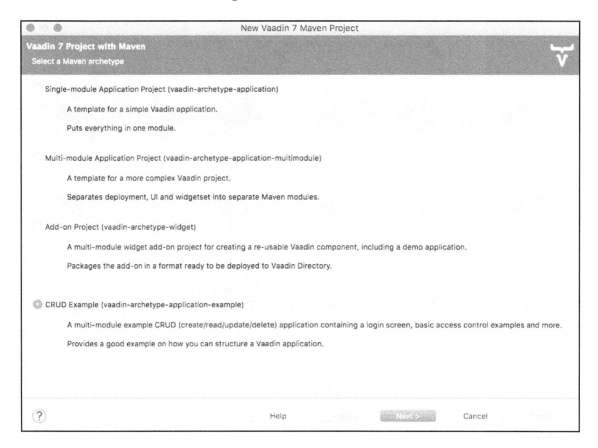

7. The Vaadin sample application gets created and is shown in your Eclipse **Project Explorer**, as shown in the following screenshot. This is a multi-module Vaadin application:

 We will not go into the details of this application. We will use this as a sample application with a web interface, which will authenticate users using the application's own login module, and we will see how we can bind a Single Sign On authentication service to decouple the user authentication functionality from the application logic.

8. Now, to be able to build this Vaadin application locally, you will need to have the Maven plugin installed in Eclipse.

 You can also choose to have Maven installed locally on your machine and build the application from your terminal window.
Download the latest version of Maven from https://maven.apache.org/

download.cgi.

Follow the installation instructions for your OS, as explained at https://m aven.apache.org/install.html.

9. For details on the Maven plugin for Eclipse and for help with installing it, you can refer to https://marketplace.eclipse.org/content/maven-integration-eclipse-luna-and-newer.

You can also install the Maven plugin for Eclipse from **Help** | **Eclipse Marketplace** in your Eclipse.

10. Before you can deploy the application on Bluemix, you will need to build the application locally to create the deployable .war file. Instructions in this section will assume that you have the Eclipse plugin for Maven installed.

If you are using Maven locally, outside of Eclipse, you will need to adapt the following instructions appropriately and use the mvn commands.

11. Expand the sample Vaadin application created. You will find the `pom.xml` file, which contains the build definitions for Maven. Right-click on the `pom.xml` file and select **Run As | Maven install** from the menu:

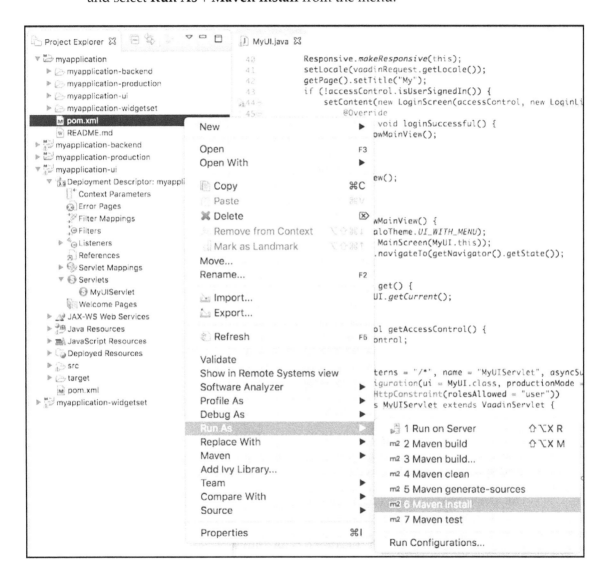

Once the build runs successfully, you will see the deployable `.war` file created under the `target` folder, as shown in the following screenshot:

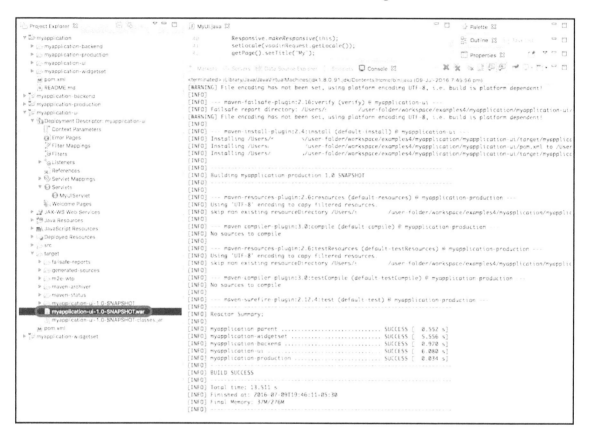

12. Now to deploy the application to Bluemix. Go to the `cf` command line and execute the following command, after logging in to your Bluemix organization and space (where you have created the Single Sign On service):

```
cf push <unique-application-name>
   -p myapplication-ui-1.0-SNAPSHOT.war
```

An example command for this demo is as follows:

```
cf push myvaadinapp-b05307 -p myapplication-ui-1.0-SNAPSHOT.war
```

Make sure you change the directory in your terminal window to the folder where the deployable `.war` file is.

13. Successful execution of the preceding command will deploy the Vaadin application on Bluemix and start it. The dump of the command execution is as shown in the following screenshot:

```
$ cf push myvaadinapp-b05307 -p myapplication-ui-1.0.SNAPSHOT.war
Creating app myvaadinapp-b05307 in org
OK

Creating route myvaadinapp-b05307.mybluemix.net...
OK

Binding myvaadinapp-b05307.mybluemix.net to myvaadinapp-b05307...
OK

Uploading myvaadinapp-b05307...
Uploading app files from: /var/folders/81/g_8p5x257c3bjjsbmfmymyf80000gq/T/unzipped-app008060618
Uploading 1.5M, 77 files
Done uploading
OK

Starting app myvaadinapp-b05307 in org
-----> Downloaded app package (28M)
-----> Liberty Buildpack Version: v3.0-20160608-1450
-----> Retrieving IBM 1.8.0_20160428 JRE (ibm-java-jre-8.0-3.0-pxa6480sr3-20160428_01-cloud.tgz) ... (0.0s)
       Expanding JRE to .java ... (1.0s)
-----> Retrieving App Management 1.17.0_20160418-1204 (app-mgmt_v1.17-20160418-1204.zip) ... (0.0s)
       Expanding App Management to .app-management (0.1s)
-----> Retrieving com.ibm.ws.liberty-16.0.0.2-201606081450.tar.gz ... (0.0s)
       Installing archive ... (1.0s)
-----> Warning: Liberty feature set is not specified. Using the default feature set: ["beanValidation-1.1", "cdi-1.2", "ejbLite-3.2", "el-3.0", "jaxrs-2.0", "jdbc-4.1",
"jndi-1.0", "jpa-2.1", "jsf-2.2", "jsonp-1.0", "jsp-2.3", "managedBeans-1.0", "servlet-3.1", "websocket-1.1"]. For the best results, explicitly set the features via the
JBP_CONFIG_LIBERTY environment variable or deploy the application as a server directory or packaged server with a custom server.xml file.
-----> Liberty buildpack is done creating the droplet

-----> Uploading droplet (147M)

0 of 1 instances running, 1 starting
0 of 1 instances running, 1 starting
1 of 1 instances running

App started

OK

App myvaadinapp-b05307 was started using this command `.liberty/initial_startup.rb`

Showing health and status for app myvaadinapp-b05307 in                                       ...
OK

requested state: started
instances: 1/1
usage: 1G x 1 instances
urls: myvaadinapp-b05307.mybluemix.net
last uploaded: Sun Jul 10 02:46:00 UTC 2016
stack: unknown
buildpack: Liberty for Java(TM) (WAR, liberty-16.0.0.2, buildpack-v3.0-20160608-1450, ibmjdk-1.8.0_20160428, env)

     state      since                    cpu       memory          disk          details
#0   running    2016-07-10 08:17:17 AM   280.4%    218.9M of 1G    201.2M of 1G
```

14. Now you access your application using the application route or URL, which in the case of this demonstration is `https://myvaadinapp-b537.mybluemix.net`.

15. You will see the application login screen, which is part of the authentication functionality built into the application:

16. We see that this sample application allows for an admin user to log in with any password, so let us type the username as `admin` and password as `admin`, and click **Login**. Once logged in, you will see an inventory of products, as shown in the following screenshot. You can perform **CRUD** (**create, retrieve, update, and delete**) operations on the products here:

Let us now look at how to integrate the Single Sign On service in Bluemix with your application so that the user authentication functionality is decoupled from your application. You can use the plug and play approach to build user authentication into your application.

Modify the sample application to enable the use of the Single Sign On service

In this section, we will learn about the minor changes that should be incorporated into the application code and deployment artifacts so that the security constraints are defined.

We will see how to define servlet security using annotations:

1. In Eclipse, go to your application servlet definition. Open the file, `MyUI.java`, present at `myapplication-ui/src/main/java/com/example/myapplication/samples/`.

If your JEE application has a `web.xml` file, you can define servlet security in the `web.xml` file as well.

2. Go to the bottom of the class where `MyUIServlet` is defined. Add the `ServletSecurity` annotation to the servlet definition, as shown here:

```
@ServletSecurity(@HttpConstraint(rolesAllowed = {"user"}))
    public static class MyUIServlet extends VaadinServlet {
    }
```

This annotation ensures that all HTTP methods on the servlet are securely accessible by users whose roles are defined as user.

3. We will need to make one more change in the `MyUI.java` file. Earlier, we discussed that what we want to eventually achieve is to replace the authentication function in the application with Single Sign On. So, let us comment out the piece of code that shows the user login screen when the application URL is launched (Screenshot in Step 15 of previous section). The following is the code change in the `init` method:

```
@Override
protected void init(VaadinRequest vaadinRequest) {
  Responsive.makeResponsive(this);
  setLocale(vaadinRequest.getLocale());
  getPage().setTitle("MyVaadinApp");
```

```
    showMainView();
    /*if (!accessControl.isUserSignedIn()) {
      setContent(new LoginScreen(accessControl, new LoginListener() {
        @Override
        public void loginSuccessful() {
          showMainView();
        }
      }));
    } else {
      showMainView();
    }*/
  }
```

4. You will see that in the code snippet, we have commented out the portion where the login screen is displayed for user login. We will go directly to the application page where the inventory is displayed (`showMainView();`). Save the file.

5. Now we will need to make one more change to a deployment artifact, which is in `ibm-application-bnd.xml`. Create the `myapplication-ui/src/main/webapp/META-INF/ibm-application-bnd.xml` file.

6. Copy the following contents to the `ibm-application-bnd.xml` file:

```
<?xml version="1.0" encoding="UTF-8"?>
<application-bnd xmlns:xsi=
  "http://www.w3.org/2001/XMLSchema-instance"
  xmlns="http://websphere.ibm.com/xml/ns/javaee"
  xsi:schemaLocation="http://websphere.ibm.com/xml/ns/javaee
http://websphere.ibm.com/xml/ns/javaee/ibm-application-bnd_1_0.xsd"
  version="1.0">
  <security-role name="user">
    <special-subject type="ALL_AUTHENTICATED_USERS"/>
  </security-role>
</application-bnd>
```

7. Save the file. Now let us build a new war file and update the application deployment on Bluemix. Right-click on the `pom.xml` file under `myapplication`, as explained earlier. Select **Run As | Maven clean**. This will remove the `.war` file that was created previously.

8. Now select **Run As | Maven install**, on the `pom.xml` file under `myapplication`.

9. Once the build runs successfully, you will see the deployable `.war` file created under the `target` folder.

10. To deploy the application to Bluemix, go to the cf command line and execute the following command, after logging in to your Bluemix organization and space (where you have the Single Sign On service created):

```
cf push <unique-application-name> -p
   myapplication-ui-1.0-SNAPSHOT.war
```

Example command for this demo is as follows:

```
cf push myvaadinapp-b05307 -p myapplication-ui-1.0-SNAPSHOT.war
```

Make sure you change directory in your terminal window to the folder
where the deployable .war file is.

11. Successful execution of the preceding command will update the Vaadin
    application on Bluemix and start it. The dump of the command execution is as
    shown in the following screenshot:

```
● ● ●                                    target — -bash — 169×57
                                    $ cf push myvaadinapp-b05307 -p myapplication-ui-1.0-SNAPSHOT.war
Updating app myvaadinapp-b05307 in org                                              ...
OK

Uploading myvaadinapp-b05307...
Uploading app files from: /var/folders/81/q_8p5x257c3bjjsbmfmymyf80000gq/T/unzipped-app951561899
Uploading 424.2K, 77 files
Done uploading
OK

Stopping app myvaadinapp-b05307 in org                                              ...
OK

Starting app myvaadinapp-b05307 in org                                              ...
-----> Downloaded app package (20M)
-----> Downloaded app buildpack cache (4.0K)
-----> Liberty Buildpack Version: v3.0-20160608-1450
-----> Retrieving IBM 1.8.0_20160428 JRE (ibm-java-jre-8.0-3.0 pxa6480sr3-20160428_01-cloud.tgz) ... (0.0s)
       Expanding JRE to .java ... (1.0s)
-----> Retrieving App Management 1.17.0_20160418-1204 (app-mgmt_v1.17 20160418-1204.zip) ... (0.0s)
       Expanding App Management to .app-management (0.1s)
-----> Retrieving com.ibm.ws.liberty-16.0.0.2-201606081450.tar.gz ... (0.0s)
       Installing archive ... (1.0s)
-----> Warning: Liberty feature set is not specified. Using the default feature set: ["beanValidation-1.1", "cdi-1.2", "ejbLite-3.2", "el-3.0", "jaxrs-2.0", "jdbc-4.1",
"jndi-1.0", "jpa-2.1", "jsf-2.2", "jsonp-1.0", "jsp-2.3", "managedBeans-1.0", "servlet-3.1", "websocket-1.1"]. for the best results, explicitly set the features via the
JBP_CONFIG_LIBERTY environment variable or deploy the application as a server directory or packaged server with a custom server.xml file.
-----> Auto-configuration is creating config for service instance 'Single Sign On-vt' of type 'SingleSignOn'
-----> Liberty buildpack is done creating the droplet

-----> Uploading droplet (147M)

0 of 1 instances running, 1 starting
0 of 1 instances running, 1 starting
0 of 1 instances running, 1 starting
1 of 1 instances running

App started

OK

App myvaadinapp-b05307 was started using this command '.liberty/initial_startup.rb'

Showing health and status for app myvaadinapp-b05307 in org                         ...
OK

requested state: started
instances: 1/1
usage: 1G x 1 instances
urls: myvaadinapp-b05307.mybluemix.net
last uploaded: Mon Jul 11 07:22:08 UTC 2016
stack: unknown
buildpack: Liberty for Java(TM) (WAR, liberty-16.0.0_2, buildpack-v3.0-20160608-1450, ibmjdk-1.8.0_20160428, env)

     state      since                 cpu      memory         disk        details
#0   running    2016-07-11 12:53:41 PM   1.8%    224.7M of 1G   201.6M of 1G
```

Now our application is updated with the changes we made. The next step is to bind the
Single Sign On service to your application.

Integrating the Single Sign On service with your application

Once your application is ready and your Single Sign On service is configured and bound to your application, it is time to integrate the service to your application. Follow the steps in this section to integrate the configured Single Sign On service to your application:

1. Go to your application from the Bluemix dashboard and click the application tile:

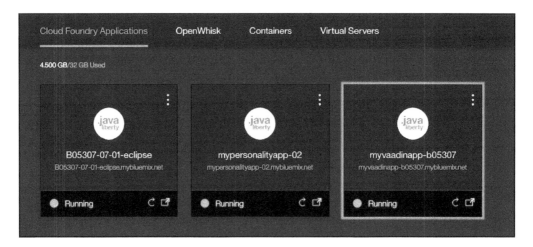

2. Go to the **Connections** view for your application, as shown in the following screenshot:

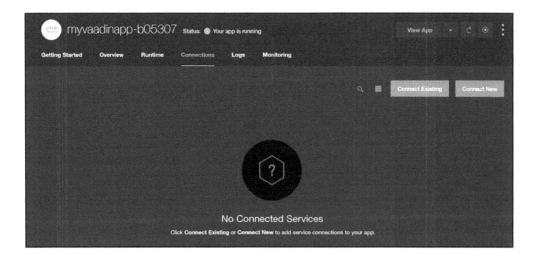

3. Since we have already created and configured the Single Sign On service, click **Connect Existing**.

4. This will display the existing services within your Bluemix organization and space. Choose the Single Sign On service instance and click **Connect**:

4. You will be prompted to restage your application during the binding of the service to the application. Click **Restage**:

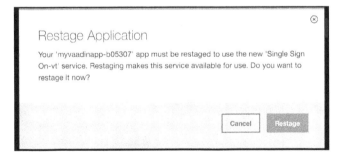

5. When your application is getting restaged, you can look at the logs by going to the **Logs** view, as shown in the following screenshot:

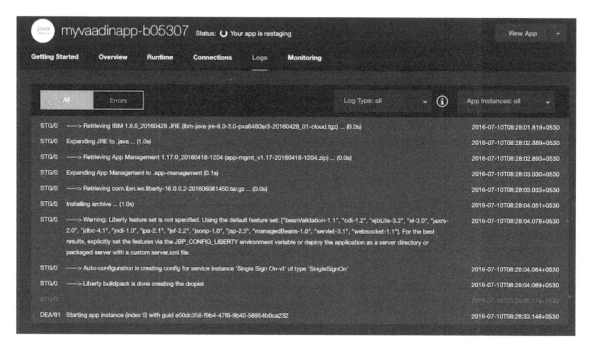

6. After the application is successfully restaged, you will see the Single Sign On service instance under the **Connections** view for your application, as shown in the following screenshot:

7. Click the service tile from under the **Connections** view to open the Single Sign On service dashboard. We will now integrate the service to work with your application.

8. You will now see an **Integrate** tab. Click on **Integrate** to configure the integration between the Single Sign On service and your application:

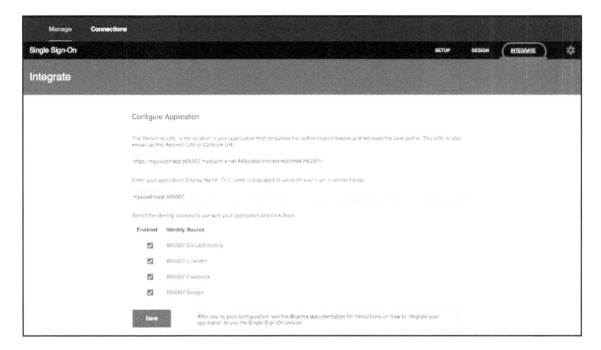

9. You will see a default callback URL. Leave it unchanged. You can choose to use any or all of the configured identity sources for your application by unchecking or checking the identity sources listed.

For this demo, let us choose to only have two identity sources supported for your application, which are Cloud Directory and LinkedIn:

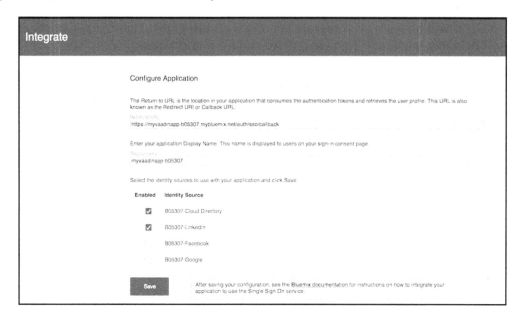

10. Click **Save**. The following prompt indicates successful configuration. Click **OK**:

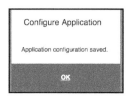

Seeing it all work together

Let us now see in action how the Single Sign On authentication service is leveraged to authenticate users to your web application:

1. Go to your application URL. In the case of this demonstration, it is `https://myva` `adinapp-b537.mybluemix.net`.

2. You will see an automatic redirection of the application URL in the browser address bar. You will now see the screen shown in the following screenshot:

3. You will see that the user of your application is now shown two login options: they can now sign in using a cloud directory or LinkedIn account, both of which are the configured identity sources in your Single Sign On service.

4. Now, as a user, let us select **Sign in with B05307-Cloud Directory**:

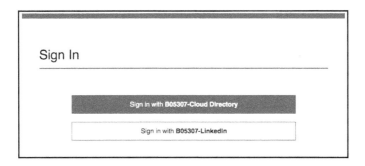

5. You will now be shown the screen shown in the following screenshot, where you can enter the username and password. The user name and password are validated against the cloud directory you have created in the Single Sign On service:

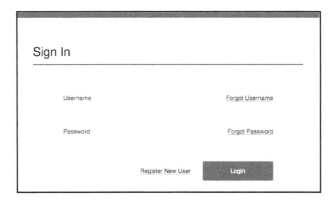

6. Enter the credentials for one of the users we created while configuring **B05307-Cloud Directory** in the Single Sign On service:

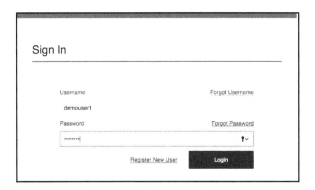

7. Click **Login**. You will see that you are taken directly to the product inventory list:

8. Now let us clear the browser cache and attempt to launch the application URL again. This time, select **Sign in with B05307-LinkedIn**:

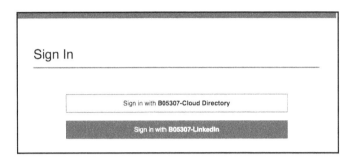

9. You will get the following prompt to enter your LinkedIn credentials:

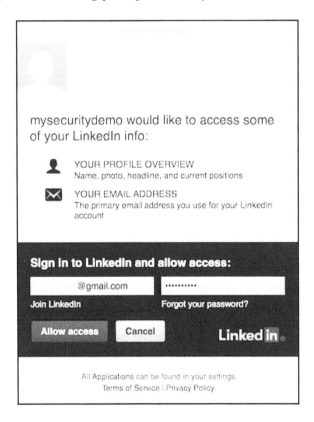

10. Enter your LinkedIn credentials and click **Allow access**. As seen in previous steps, the name of the application used in this demo to register the application in LinkedIn is `mysecuritydemo`.

11. You will see that you are taken directly to the product inventory list:

12. You can go back to the Single Sign On service dashboard from the **Connections** view in your application details screen and from the Integrate tab, you can check to include Google+ as another identity source for your application.

13. If you launch your application URL, you will now see the additional option of using Google+ for authentication to your application. Select **Sign in with B05307-Google**:

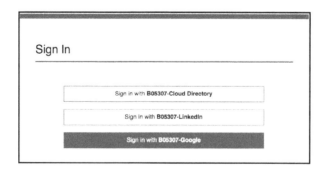

14. You will be prompted to enter your Google user credentials:

15. You will see that you are taken directly to the product inventory list:

Summary

In this chapter, we discussed the security services available in Bluemix and we delved deeper into using two of the available security services in Bluemix. We learned how to offload your web application authentication functionality to the Single Sign On service in Bluemix. We also learned how to configure different kinds of identity sources in Single Sign On, and saw how they can be integrated to work with your application running on Bluemix.

In the next chapter, we will learn about microservice architecture and why Bluemix is a great platform for building applications that use microservice architecture.

9
Microservices-based Application Development on Bluemix

In this chapter, we will learn about an architecture pattern for application development on cloud, called the microservices architecture pattern. We will also learn how to use Bluemix, and services on Bluemix, to build and deploy applications that employ the microservices architecture. In a nutshell, we will learn about the following topics:

- Understanding the microservices architecture pattern
- Developing a microservice-based application on Bluemix.

Understanding the microservices architecture pattern

The microservices architecture pattern is a method to develop applications that are composed of smaller applications, each of which is developed as a small service and has independent lifecycle management. These smaller services are loosely coupled together to form a larger application. When you consider whether an application should use microservices architecture, you should carefully evaluate whether it makes sense for the smaller functions to exist as independent microservices. Since each of the constituent microservices in a microservices-based application has its own lifecycle management, you will have DevOps for each of the services managed independently.

One of the things you need to consider before you break your application down into microservices is the granularity required. Breaking it down into too many granular units would increase the operations overhead, while breaking it down into too few units would increase the application's complexity and failure points. Careful consideration of the requirements, outcome, and operations overhead would need to be taken before any application can be considered for design using a microservices pattern.

In a microservices pattern, each of the services should be able to achieve a certain viable functional completeness. The means to share data between each of these microservices will have to be consistent and reliable, and independent of any failures that may occur in any of the constituent microservices at any point in time.

This architectural pattern is a very useful pattern for application development on cloud platforms such as Bluemix. Application developers can now leverage portions of functionality from value-added services on such cloud platforms and can build only the application logic that is required for their business. This expedites application development timelines and provides the impetus required to bring innovative applications to the market faster than would otherwise be the case.

The following screenshot shows the visual representation of what a monolithic application is, as opposed to what a microservices-based application is:

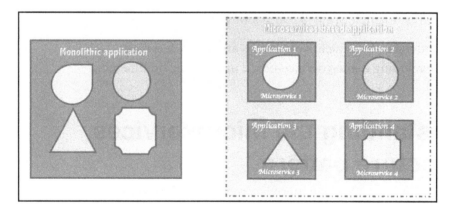

You will see that the monolithic application has all the necessary functionality built into the same deployable module or unit, which eventually runs on the same infrastructure. However, in the case of a microservices-based application, you will see that each of the functions of the application is broken down as a deployable application unit, and each of them can run in their own infrastructure. The failure of one microservice does not bring all the other microservices down. The composition of individual microservices forms the new microservice-based application.

Since each of the microservices is a deployable unit by itself and has an independent and individual DevOps, or lifecycle, you will notice that each of the microservices can also be scaled individually, as opposed to the need to scale the entire application, in the case of a monolithic application. This gives the ability to only scale those services that consume greater resources with increase in load. Microservices that are low or static in resource consumption in response to load increase or decrease can be configured to scale to a lesser number of nodes, or can afford to not have additional nodes associated, as shown in the following screenshot:

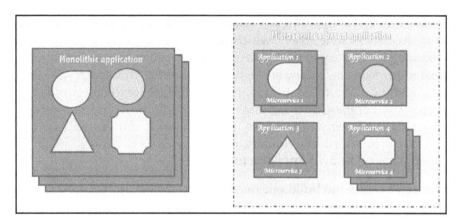

 There are various published resources on microservices architecture; you can refer to them for detailed understanding of this pattern. Some of the resources you can use are
http://microservices.io/patterns/microservices.html and http://ma
rtinfowler.com/articles/microservices.html.

Developing a microservices-based application on Bluemix

Having gained an understanding of what Bluemix is and what it offers from the previous chapters, and now having gained an understanding of the microservices pattern, you will be able to get a perspective on why Bluemix is a platform that is suitable for microservices-based application development. Let us immediately get into discussing an application use case that we will illustrate in this section, which will also help to bring forth the concept of microservices and help with your understanding of this.

In this section, we will build an application leveraging concepts and applications that we have developed and learned in previous chapters. We will be using the application we developed in Chapter 4, *Leveraging On-Premise Software for Applications on Bluemix* in which we retrieved a certain Twitter feed, translated it into French, did some sentiment analysis on it, and then persisted it in a MongoDB database that existed locally on your workstation. This will form one application, or microservice, for us. Next, we will build another application, which will retrieve persisted negative tweets from MongoDB (which is updated by our first microservice). We will augment the tweets retrieved by first translating them back to English, and then we will use the cognitive function of tone analysis to find the social tone scores for each of the retrieved tweets. We will then create a formatted output of the tweets with their social tone scores, which will be obtained by a user sending an HTTP request. At the same time, we will have this application call out to an OpenWhisk trigger, which we created in Chapter 7, *Compute Options on Bluemix*. This application will be our microservice 2, and the OpenWhisk trigger, which will execute a configured action, will be our microservice 3. All of these microservices together will form our microservices based application. As we can see, each of the three microservices in our example are independent deployable units, can be scaled individually, can run without dependencies on each other, and each of them runs on its own infrastructure units.

Let us now go step by step and build our microservices-based application.

Microservice 1

The first microservice for this illustration is the application you built in Chapter 4, *Leveraging On-Premise Software for Applications on Bluemix*. We will not be going over the steps for building this application again in this section. If you followed Chapter 4, *Leveraging On-Premise Software for Applications on Bluemix*, before reaching here, then you will already have this application deployed in your Bluemix account. If not, please go back to Chapter 4, *Leveraging On-Premise Software for Applications on Bluemix*, follow the steps to create the application that retrieves tweets from the configured Twitter stream, analyzes the tweet sentiment, separates out the negative-sentiment tweets, and persists them in MongoDB, which is configured on a local system.

Let us now proceed to the next section, assuming you have this step completed and microservice 1 is available to you.

Microservice 3

Before going into the development of microservice 2, let us make sure we have microservice 3 available. If you followed `Chapter 7`, *Compute Options on Bluemix*, before reaching here, you will already have created the `OpenWhisk Cloudant` trigger, any action that needs to occur when the trigger occurs, and finally, the rule that associates the trigger and the action.

In the action, we will make a small modification for this example, since the `Cloudant` trigger that will invoke this action will not be returning an `_id`, which we used to print in the action when we executed it in the example in `Chapter 7`, *Compute Options on Bluemix*. We will modify the action to just print a string to indicate that the trigger, called from our microservice 2, has executed the action code.

The action code from `Chapter 7`, *Compute Options on Bluemix*, will be as shown in the following screenshot:

We will be modifying it to look like the following screenshot. Click **Make it Live** once you have edited the action code:

 You can customize the action code to do anything useful that you want. We are using this simple action merely to illustrate the functionality and method of using OpenWhisk applications.

Let us go into the next part of this illustration, which is to create microservice 2.

 If you have not followed the OpenWhisk example in Chapter 7, *Compute Options on Bluemix*, please go back to Chapter 7, *Compute Options on Bluemix*, and create the trigger, action, and rule as explained there. This is required before you can follow the steps to create microservice 2.

Microservice 2

Please follow the steps in this section only after you have completed the sections on microservice 1 and microservice 3.

Let us now create a new application that will act as microservice 2 in our illustration of a microservices-based application. Follow the steps given here to create the application:

1. Log in to Bluemix and on the welcome page, click **Compute**:

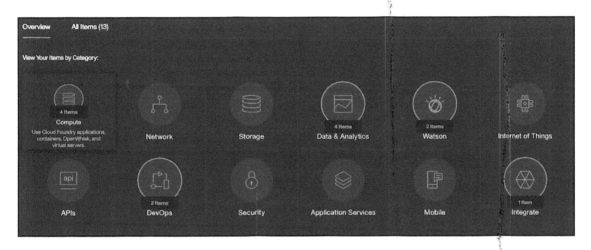

2. Click on the icon highlighted in the following screenshot to take you to the options available on Bluemix to create a Cloud Foundry application:

3. Select the **Node-RED Starter** boilerplate, as shown in the following screenshot:

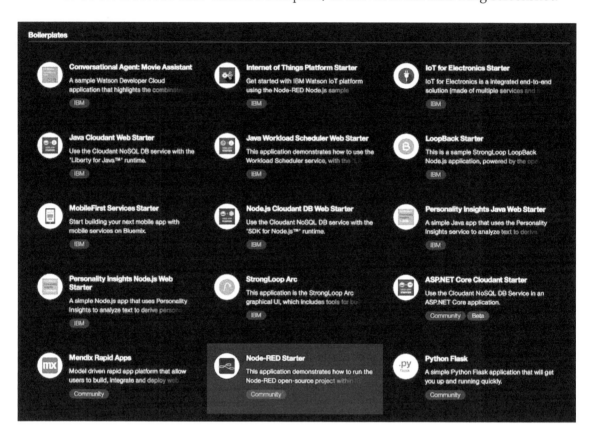

4. Give your application a name, review the plans for the services that come with the boilerplate, and click **Create**:

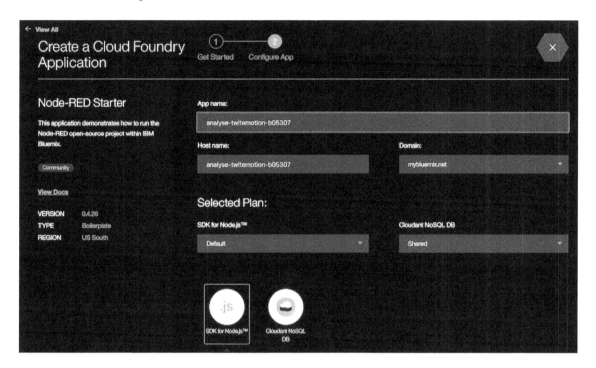

5. Once your application is created and has started successfully, you will see it in the dashboard, as shown in the following screenshot. Click **Open URL** to go to the Node-RED editor, from where you can start wiring your application functionality:

6. Click **Go to your Node-RED flow editor**:

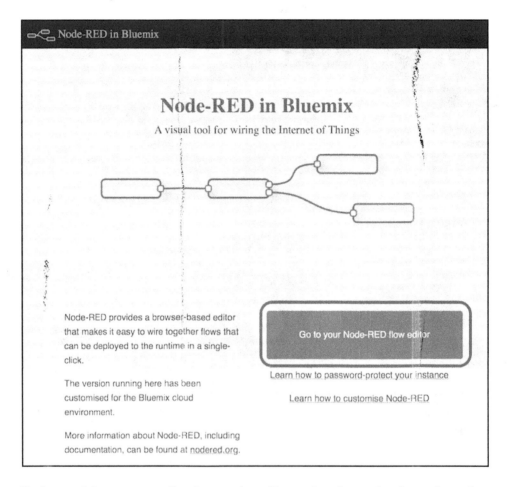

7. Start wiring your application on the editor using the nodes from the palette on the left.

8. We will first wire the flow with the nodes that we need. Then we will learn to configure each of these nodes individually. The flow we will wire for this application is as shown in the following screenshot:

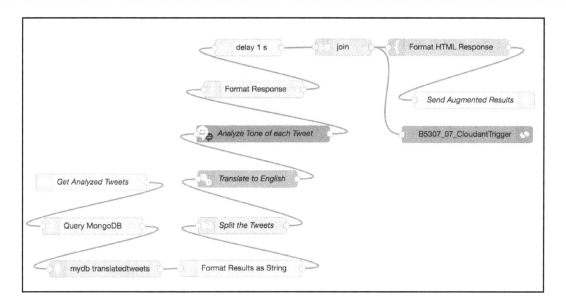

Wiring and configuring the flow

Let us learn to wire and configure the flow:

1. Drag and drop an **http** input node from the nodes palette onto your empty editor pane:

2. Double-click on the **http** node to configure it, then give the node a name and a URL, which will be used by the application user to trigger the flow we will be wiring in the application. Ensure the HTTP method is selected as **GET**:

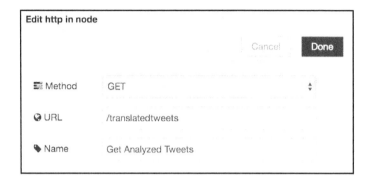

3. Next, drag and drop a **function** node from the nodes palette:

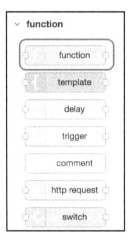

4. Double-click the **function** node to configure it. Give the node a name, such as Query MongoDB, as this is the node where we will be defining some of the parameters that are necessary to build the query to retrieve stored records from MongoDB. As seen in the following screenshot, we are restricting the number of records returned by the query by defining msg.limit. Here, we have limited it to 30 records. Next, we want the query to fetch the last few records each time it is run, so we will ensure this happens by defining msg.sort. We can also choose to just get the payload field from the query and can ignore the other fields by defining msg.projection, as shown in the following screenshot:

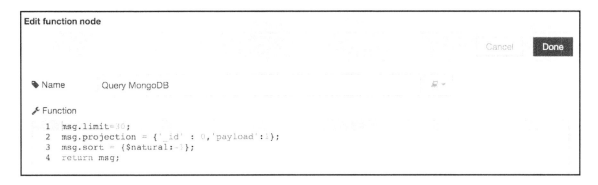

Edit function node

Cancel   Done

🏷 Name   Query MongoDB

🔧 Function

```
1   msg.limit=30;
2   msg.projection = {'_id' : 0,'payload':1};
3   msg.sort = {$natural:-1};
4   return msg;
```

5. Wire the **http** and **function** nodes together. Next, drag and drop the **mongodb** node from the palette, shown in the following screenshot:

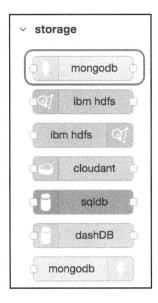

6. Double-click on the **mongodb** node to configure it. Since this node is going to query MongoDB to fetch data, make sure you set the **Operation** field as **find**. Provide the **Server** and **Collection** information as configured in `Chapter 4`, *Leveraging On-Premise Software for Applications on Bluemix*, when configuring the MongoDB node in the application:

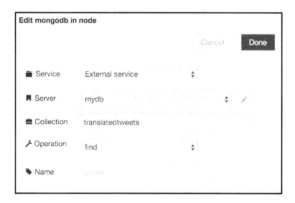

7. Your server configuration should look like that shown in the following screenshot, similar to how we had configured it in `Chapter 4`, *Leveraging On-Premise Software for Applications on Bluemix*, when configuring the mongodb node. Make sure you are selecting the same database that was used in the application (microservice 1) to persist translated tweets:

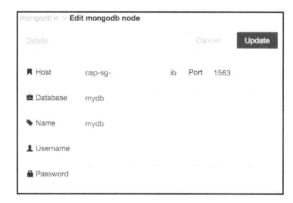

8. Now wire the configured**mongodb** node to the **function** node, as shown in the following screenshot:

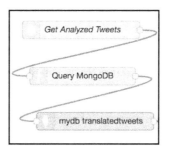

To test the flow when you are wiring it, attach a **debug** node to the output of the last node in the flow and see the output in the debug console.

To invoke the flow, you can go to a browser and access the GET URL of the HTTP node you have configured in the flow. For this illustration, it would be

```
https://analyse-twitemotion-b05307.mybluemix.net/translat
edtweets.
```

9. If you deploy and run the flow we have created so far, we will get an output such as that shown here, which is the payload field for 30 documents from MongoDB:

```
[ { "payload": "Ce clown a manifestementjamaisentenduparler del'
  expression "vide clang plus les navires"
  https://t.co/YTM6brhVSQ" },
  { "payload": "@revieweroPeut-êtreelleestmelo-dramatizing pour son
    incapacité à effectueren raison de problèmesd'aptitude sur ce
    jour @narendramodi" },
  { "payload": "RT @PMOIndia: attristépar la perte de vies due à un
    séismeenItalie. Condoléances aux famillesendeuillées&prières avec
    les blessés: PM @nar ..." },
  { "payload": "@14Mohjas RT: JungleRaj Au
    Gujarat\n@narendramodisivous
    ne pouvez pas contrôler les troubles
    sociauxdanstoutel'Indevousdevezvolunteerlydémissionner." },
  { "payload": "@daveakash2 RT: aucune accusation de sédition sur
    @narendramodi n @manoharparrikar???
    #NavyInfoLeaksParrikarSleeps" },
  { "payload": "@HemantNoida2015 RT: @yadavakhileshacheteursjaha Sir
    ye #kaisaPradeshUttar Pradesh# korahehaiaurpilleraucune action
```

```
            de côtéur. Https:/ ..." },
        { "payload": "@narendramodi l ....]
```

10. You will notice that we are indeed getting the tweets in French from our MongoDB (inserted into the database by microservice 1). Let us proceed further with our application (microservice 2) and try to format the results in such a way that we can do more augmentation on the data retrieved. Continuing with our application build, let us drag and drop another function node to the editor. Double-click on it to write the code that will format the results:

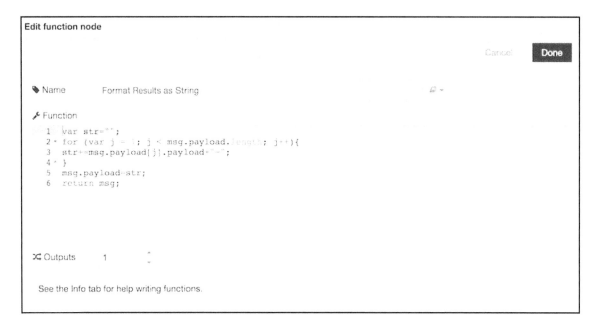

The code entered in the preceding function node is provided as follows:

```
varstr="";
for (var j = 1; j <msg.payload.length; j++){
  str+=msg.payload[j].payload+"~";
}
msg.payload=str;
return msg;
```

11. You will now see the post execution of the flow, the output being one string with all the tweets separated by "~" (which was set in the code), as shown in the following screenshot of the debug console:

msg.payload : string [4133]

@reviewero Peut-être elle est melo-dramatizing pour son incapacité à effectuer en raison de problèmes d'aptitude sur ce jour @narendramodi~RT @PMOIndia: attristé par la perte de vies due à un séisme en Italie. Condoléances aux familles endeuillées & prières avec les blessés: PM @nar ...~@14Mohjas RT: JungleRaj Au Gujarat @narendramodi si vous ne pouvez pas contrôler les troubles sociaux dans toute l'Inde vous devez volunteerly démissionner.~@daveakash2 RT: aucune accusation de sédition sur @narendramodi n @manoharparrikar??? #NavyInfoLeaksParrikarSleeps~@HemantNoida2015 RT: @yadavakhilesh acheteurs jaha Sir ye #kaisaPradeshUttar Pradesh# ko rahe hai aur piller aucune action de côté ur. Https:/ ...~@narendramodi l'eau de drainage rempli de déchets eau & fr toutes maisons & hôtels + septicTanks scellés tous sur les moustiques et le paludisme Inde =~@HemantNoida2015 RT: @narendramodi @yadavakhilesh Sir pourquoi nous punir quand nous ne faisons pas quelque chose de mal. Kab ....

12. Now to be able to do any kind of analysis or augmentation of the results, we will need to split the results into individual tweets. For this, drag and drop the **split** node to the editor and wire it to the function node we created in the previous step:

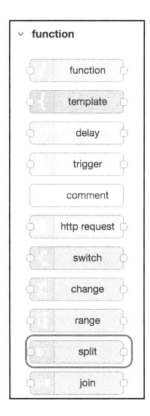

13. You will now see the post execution of the flow, the output being individual tweets set as a string onto `msg.payload`, in the flow:

msg.payload : string [143]

@HemantNoida2015 RT: @yadavakhilesh acheteurs jaha Sir ye #kaisaPradeshUttar Pradesh# ko rahe hai aur piller aucune action de côté ur. Https:/ ...

msg.payload : string [150]

@narendramodi l'eau de drainage rempli de déchets eau & fr toutes maisons & hôtels + septicTanks scellés tous sur les moustiques et le paludisme Inde =

msg.payload : string [166]

@HemantNoida2015 RT: @narendramodi @yadavakhilesh Sir pourquoi nous punir quand nous ne faisons pas quelque chose de mal. Kab khaomoshi toroge Akhilesh ji https ...

msg.payload : string [140]

@manoharparrikar @narendramodi @rajnathsingh चाहे Scorpians Submirine का Production बंद करना पड़े पर Data fuite करनेवाला चोर छुटना नहीं चाहिये

msg.payload : string [184]

@shammybaweja RT: Mufti décédé plaidé avec @narendramodi pour être un Vajpayee. Est-ce que prendre plus de lingo-insaniyat et jhamooriyat-être en soi ...

msg.payload : string [158]

@shammybaweja RT: 'Tous les Indiens aime' Cachemire dit @narendramodi Étant donné la virulence pure sur @TwitterIndia je suis certain à mort il n'est pas ...

msg.payload : string [90]

Sous-marin Scorpène données fuite https://t.co/U6xkC8PwQ4 @narendramodi @Swamy39 @RatanSharda55

msg.payload : string [134]

@rajs66 RT: Aucune surprise, @narendramodi a fait la vie pour @INCIndia un enfer. Ils sont tenus de pleurer. Https://t.co/dOt2VggUWz

msg.payload : string [150]

RT @PMOIndia: attristé par la perte de vies due à un séisme en Italie. Condoléances aux familles endeuillées & prières avec les blessés: PM @nar ...

Now we will make use of value-added services from Bluemix, which in their own capacity can be considered as additional microservices that would make up this application. For the sake of this discussion, we will just call them Bluemix services. So, in this application, we want to convert the tweet text back to English, so we will use the **language translation** node, such as the one we used in `Chapter 4`, *Leveraging On-Premise Software for Applications on Bluemix*, for our microservice 1 application. Here, the assumption is that you already have the Watson Language Translation service added to your Bluemix account, which you would have done in `Chapter 4`, *Leveraging On-Premise Software for Applications on Bluemix*.

14. Drag and drop the **language translation** node to the current flow, double-click on the node to configure it, use the credentials from the service in your Bluemix account, and choose **English** as **Target** and **French** as **Source**:

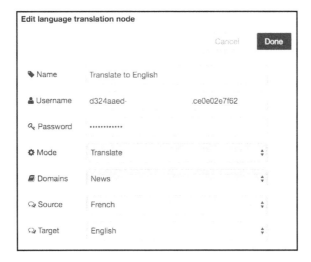

15. Wire the **language translation** node to the **split** node. Deploy and execute the flow by hitting the http **GET URL** of the **http** input node, you will see the following output in the debug console:

msg.payload : string [67]

@JPNadda @narendramodi Rehabilitation expected since 18 months https://t.co/OUC8CME3Gk

msg.payload : string [133]

@shammybaweja RT: 'All Indians love' Kashmir said @narendramodi Given the virulence pure @TwitterIndia I am sure to death is not ...

msg.payload : string [149]

RT @PMOIndia: saddened by the loss of life due to earthquake in Italy. Condolences to bereaved families & prayers with the injured: PM @nar ...

msg.payload : string [116]

@ajitasharma RT: Where is a man conman will in this case that hard-earned money is stuck! ! Https://t.co/4IfrMU90I3

msg.payload : string [149]

RT @GodrejAlpine: taxes @narendramodi paid, payment by cheque respectful of all clients. In return #godrejproperties shenanigans @ngodrej https ...

msg.payload : string [137]

@tehseenp RT: When the 'Hell' will be @manoharparrikar and India why ' Hell '@narendramodi go Pak if it is 'Hell '! Https://t.co/Mgt...

msg.payload : string [133]

RT @MahendiVora: JungleRaj In Gujarat @narendramodi if you cannot control social unrest throughout India you must volunteerly resign.

msg.payload : string [151]

@narendramodi @sardanarohit @BDUTT Itne deptt hai department in May. Itne sansad hai sab KB Department miles. They also have arms. Ek pressure pe q

msg.payload : string [141]

Without sedition charges on @narendramodi n @manoharparrikar??? #NavyInfoLeaksParrikarSleeps @IYC @_SoniaGandhi @OfficeOfRG @Bhupesh_Baghel

Next let us update the application flow to augment the results we would want to return to the user. We will use the **Watson** category service on Bluemix, **Tone Analyzer**, to analyze the tone of each of the tweet retrieved, and we will then display the tweet, along with the social tone score, for each of them.

Follow the steps given to first add the **Tone Analyzer** service instance to your Bluemix account so that you get the credentials required to configure the service in your application flow:

1. From the Bluemix welcome page, click **Watson** and then click **Tone Analyzer** from the catalog of services under the **Watson** category:

2. Give the service instance a name, review the plan details, and click **Create**:

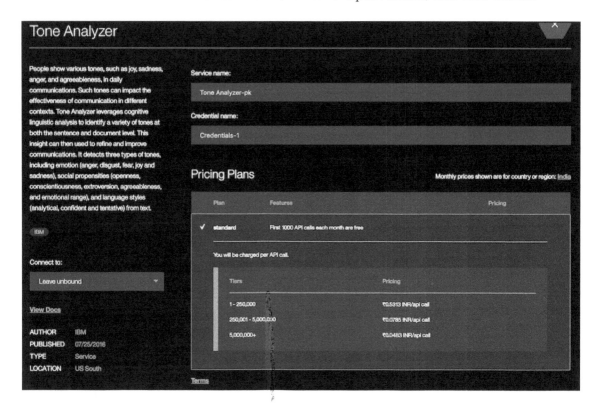

3. You will see the following service instances created on your dashboard, under the **Watson** category:

4. Click the **Tone Analyzer** tile to view the details. Go to the **Service Credentials** tab, click **View Credentials** on the credentials for the service, and make a note of the username and password, as shown in the following screenshot:

5. Go back to the Node-RED editor for your application and drag and drop the **tone analyzer v3** node from the palette:

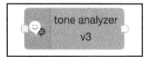

6. Double-click the node to configure it. Give the node a name and select the values as shown in the following screenshot for **Tones**, **Sentences**, and **Content Type**. Configure the **Username** and **Password** options with values obtained from the service credentials, as obtained in the previous step:

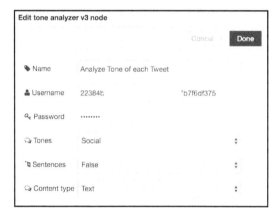

7. Wire the tone analyzer v3 node to the language translation node. Execute the flow to see the output from the tone analyzer v3 node. You will see that the output from this node is returned in `msg.response`, as shown in the following screenshot:

msg.response : Object

{ "document_tone": { "tone_categories": [{ "tones": [{ "score": 0.971, "tone_id": "openness_big5", "tone_name": "Openness" }, { "score": 0.638, "tone_id": "conscientiousness_big5", "tone_name": "Conscientiousness" }, { "score": 0.171, "tone_id": "extraversion_big5", "tone_name": "Extraversion" }, { "score": 0.068, "tone_id": "agreeableness_big5", "tone_name": "Agreeableness" }, { "score": 0.201, "tone_id": "emotional_range_big5", "tone_name": "Emotional Range" }], "category_id": "social_tone", "category_name": "Social Tone" }] } }

msg.response : Object

{ "document_tone": { "tone_categories": [{ "tones": [{ "score": 0.426, "tone_id": "openness_big5", "tone_name": "Openness" }, { "score": 0.313, "tone_id": "conscientiousness_big5", "tone_name": "Conscientiousness" }, { "score": 0.732, "tone_id": "extraversion_big5", "tone_name": "Extraversion" }, { "score": 0.103, "tone_id": "agreeableness_big5", "tone_name": "Agreeableness" }, { "score": 0.186, "tone_id": "emotional_range_big5", "tone_name": "Emotional Range" }], "category_id": "social_tone", "category_name": "Social Tone" }] } }

msg.response : Object

{ "document_tone": { "tone_categories": [{ "tones": [{ "score": 0.28, "tone_id": "openness_big5", "tone_name": "Openness" }, { "score": 0.01, "tone_id": "conscientiousness_big5", "tone_name": "Conscientiousness" }, { "score": 0.576, "tone_id": "extraversion_big5", "tone_name": "Extraversion" }, { "score": 0.042, "tone_id": "agreeableness_big5", "tone_name": "Agreeableness" }, { "score": 0.976, "tone_id": "emotional_range_big5", "tone_name": "Emotional Range" }], "category_id": "social_tone", "category_name": "Social Tone" }] } }

msg.response : Object

{ "document_tone": { "tone_categories": [{ "tones": [{ "score": 0.928, "tone_id": "openness_big5", "tone_name": "Openness" }, { "score": 0.693, "tone_id": "conscientiousness_big5", "tone_name": "Conscientiousness" }, { "score": 0.064, "tone_id": "extraversion_big5", "tone_name": "Extraversion" }, { "score": 0.004, "tone_id": "agreeableness_big5", "tone_name": "Agreeableness" }, { "score": 0.384, "tone_id": "emotional_range_big5", "tone_name": "Emotional Range" }], "category_id": "social_tone", "category_name": "Social Tone" }] } }

msg.response : Object

{ "document_tone": { "tone_categories": [{ "tones": [{ "score": 0.992, "tone_id": "openness_big5", "tone_name": "Openness" }, { "score": 0.529, "tone_id": "conscientiousness_big5", "tone_name": "Conscientiousness" }, { "score": 0.506, "tone_id": "extraversion_big5", "tone_name": "Extraversion" }, { "score": 0.121, "tone_id": "agreeableness_big5", "tone_name": "Agreeableness" }, { "score": 0.483, "tone_id": "emotional_range_big5", "tone_name": "Emotional Range" }], "category_id": "social_tone", "category_name": "Social Tone" }] } }

8. Now that we have processed each tweet retrieved, and have obtained the social tones for them, let us now format the result in such a way that we can create a display for each tweet against its social tone in a tabular format. Drag and drop a function node to the flow editor and double-click on it to add the code that will format the results, such as that shown here. The results of the execution of the flow are as shown in the debug console, as shown in the following screenshot:

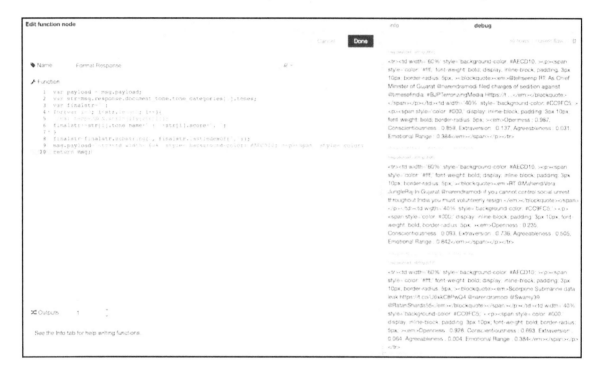

The code entered in the function node is as follows:

```
var payload = msg.payload;
varstr = msg.response.document_tone.tone_categories[0].tones;
varfinalstr = "";
for (vari = 0; i < str.length; i++) {
  finalstr += str[i].tone_name + " : " + str[i].score + ", ";
}
finalstr = finalstr.substring(0, finalstr.lastIndexOf(","));
msg.payload = "<tr><td width='60%' style='background-color: #AECD10;>
  <p><span style='color: '#fff;' font-weight: bold;
    display: inline-block; padding: 3px 10px; border-radius: 5px;'>
    <blockquote><em>" + payload + "</em></blockquote></span></p></td>
<td width='40%' style='background-color: #CC9FC5;'><p>
  <span style='color: #000;' display: inline-block;
```

```
        padding: 3px 10px; font-weight: bold; border-radius: 5px;'>
        <em>" + finalstr + "</em></span></p></tr>";
return msg;
```

9. You can add a **delay** node to introduce a small wait time till all the individual messages are available. This is optional:

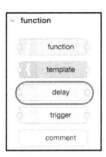

10. Next we will need to add a **join** node so that we can club the individual `msg.payload` into one `msg.payload`:

11. Double-click on the **join** node to configure it, as shown in the following screenshot. Choose the **Mode** option to be **Manual**, configure **Combine each** to **msg.payload** and **to create** to **a String**:

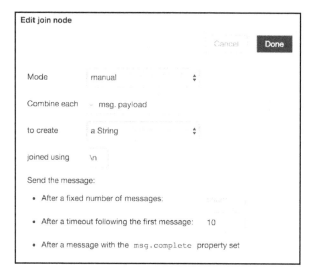

12. To embed the **msg.payload** option from the join node into an HTML page, you can drag and drop a **template** node to your flow. This is where you will write the HTML for your page containing the results:

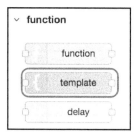

13. Double-click on the **template** node to configure it. This is where you will add the following code:

```
<style type="text/css">
    .tg    {border-collapse:collapse;border-spacing:0;
        border-color:#aaa;margin:0px auto;}
    .tg td{font-family:Arial, sans-serif;font-size:14px;
        padding:10px 5px;border-style:solid;
        border-width:1px;overflow:hidden;word-break:normal;
```

```
      border-color:#aaa;color:#333;background-color:#fff;}
   .tgth{font-family:Arial, sans-serif;font-size:14px;
     font-weight:normal;
     padding:10px 5px;border-style:solid;border-width:1px;
     overflow:hidden;word-break:normal;border-color:#aaa;
     color:#fff;background-color:#f38630;}
   .tg .tg-huo9{font-size:15px;font-family:"Lucida Console",
     Monaco, monospace !important;;vertical-align:top}
   .tg .tg-fz6y{font-size:14px;font-family:"Lucida Console",
     Monaco,  monospace !important;;vertical-align:top}
   .tg .tg-yw4l{vertical-align:top}
   th.tg-sort-header::-moz-selection { background:transparent; }
   th.tg-sort-header::selection      { background:transparent; }
   th.tg-sort-header { cursor:pointer; }table th.tg-sort-header:after
   { content:''; float:right; margin-top:7px; border-width:0 4px 4px;
     border-style:solid;  border-color:#404040 transparent;
     visibility:hidden; }
   table th.tg-sort-header:hover:after { visibility:visible; }
   table th.tg-sort-desc:after,tableth.tg-sort-asc:after,
   tableth.tg-sort-asc:hover:after { visibility:visible;
     opacity:0.4; }
   table th.tg-sort-desc:after { border-bottom:none;
     border-width:4px 4px 0;}
   @media screen and (max-width: 767px)
     {.tg {width: auto !important;}
     .tg col {width: auto !important;}.tg-wrap {overflow-x: auto;
     -webkit-overflow-scrolling: touch;margin: auto 0px;}}
</style>
<div class="tg-wrap">
  <h2 style="color: #2e6c80;">Tweets analyzed for their
    social tones:</h2>
  <table>
    </thead>
    <table id="tg-FUkU8" class="tg">
      <thead>
        <tr>
        <td style='background-color: #33314B;'>
          <center>
            <h2><b><em><font color='#fff';>Tweets</font>
              </em></b></h2>
          </center>
        </td>
        <td style='background-color: #33314B;'>
          <center>
            <h2><b><em><font color='#fff';>Social Tones</font>
              </em></b></h2>
          </center>
        </td>
```

```
        </tr>
      </thead>
    {{{payload}}}
  </table>
</div>
<script type="text/javascript" charset="utf-8">
  varTgTableSort=window.TgTableSort||function(n,t)
{"use strict";function r(n,t){for(var e=[],o=n.childNodes,i=0;
  i<o.length;++i)
{var u=o[i];if("."==t.substring(0,1)){var a=t.substring(1);
  f(u,a)&&e.push(u)}
else u.nodeName.toLowerCase()==t&&e.push(u);var c=r(u,t);e=e.concat(c)}
return e}function e(n,t)
{var e=[],o=r(n,"tr");return o.forEach(function(n)
{var o=r(n,"td");t>=0&&t<o.length&&e.push(o[t])}),e}function o(n)
{return n.textContent||n.innerText||""}function i(n)
{return n.innerHTML||""}function u(n,t){var r=e(n,t);return r.map(o)}
function a(n,t){var r=e(n,t);return r.map(i)}
function c(n){var t=n.className||"";return t.match(/\S+/g)||[]}
function f(n,t){return-1!=c(n).indexOf(t)}function s(n,t)
  {f(n,t)||(n.className+=" "+t)}
function d(n,t){if(f(n,t)){var r=c(n),e=r.indexOf(t);
  r.splice(e,1),n.className=r.join(" ")}}
function v(n){d(n,L),d(n,E)}function l(n,t,e)
  {r(n,"."+E).map(v),r(n,"."+L).map(v),e==T?s(t,E):s(t,L)}
function g(n) return function(t,r)
  {var e=n*t.str.localeCompare(r.str);
  return 0==e&&(e=t.index-r.index),e}}
function h(n){return function(t,r)
  {var e=+t.str,o=+r.str;return e==o?t.index-r.index:n*(e-o)}}
function m(n,t,r){var e=u(n,t),o=e.map(function(n,t)
  {return{str:n,index:t}}),i=e&&-1==e.map(isNaN).indexOf(!0),
  a=i?h(r):g(r);
  return o.sort(a),o.map(function(n){return n.index})}
    function p(n,t,r,o)
  {for(vari=f(o,E)?N:T,u=m(n,r,i),c=0;t>c;++c)
  {var s=e(n,c),d=a(n,c);
  s.forEach(function(n,t){n.innerHTML=d[u[t]]})}l(n,o,i)}
function x(n,t){var r=t.length;t.forEach(function(t,e)
  {t.addEventListener("click",function(){p(n,r,e,t)}),
  s(t,"tg-sort-header")})}var T=1,N=-1,E="tg-sort-asc",
  L="tg-sort-desc";return function(t){var e=n.getElementById(t),
    o=r(e,"tr"),i=o.length>0?r(o[0],"td"):[];
    0==i.length&&(i=r(o[0],"th"));
  for(var u=1;u<o.length;++u){var a=r(o[u],"td");
  if(a.length!=i.length)return}x(e,i)}}
  (document);document.addEventListener("DOMContentLoaded",function(n)
  {TgTableSort("tg-FUkU8")});
```

```
</script>
```

The payload from the previous node is embedded by means of `{{{payload}}}`, highlighted in the preceding code. This is a mustache template form for extracting **msg.payload** from the node input. Specify three pairs of braces to ensure that the HTML content that is part of the incoming **msg.payload** is not ignored.

14. Next, we are ready to complete the flow by adding an **http response** node to the flow. This is required if the flow has an HTTP input node. Drag and drop an **http response** node from the palette:

The application is almost done, but there is one thing we still want to do, which is to leverage the functionality obtained by using the `OpenWhisk` action, which is our microservice 3. Follow the steps given to build this into your application:

15. Drag and drop the **OpenWhisk** node onto your flow editor:

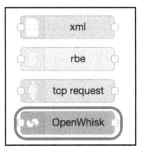

16. Double-click on the **OpenWhisk** node to configure your existing `OpenWhisk` trigger. We will be using the `B05307_07_CloudantTrigger` trigger that we configured in `Chapter 7`, *Compute Options on Bluemix*. Click the pencil icon next to **Service** to configure the OpenWhisk service:

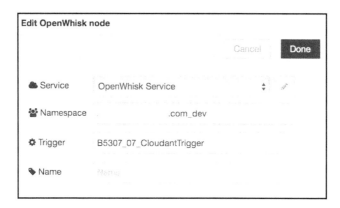

17. The configuration screen for the OpenWhisk service is as shown in the following screenshot:

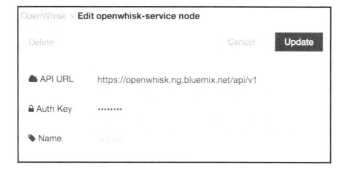

To get **Auth Key** for the OpenWhisk service, you can use the OpenWhisk CLI wsk, which was explained in `Chapter 7`, *Compute Options on Bluemix*, to execute the following command:

```
wsk property get --auth
```

Use the whisk auth key that is returned to configure the auth key in the OpenWhisk node.

Refer to `Chapter 7`, *Compute Options on Bluemix, OpenWhisk* section, for details on executing the `wsk` commands.

Similarly, to get the namespace, execute the following `wsk` command:

```
wsk property get ---namespace
```

18. Wire the configured **OpenWhisk** node to the output of the **template** node in the flow. This completes our application. The complete flow is as shown in the following screenshot:

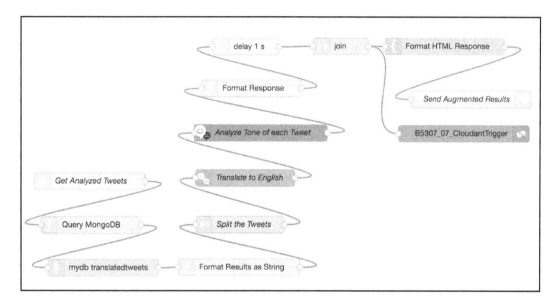

Seeing it all work together

Now we have three applications, two Cloud Foundry applications and one OpenWhisk application, running as independent applications, with their own life cycle and DevOps.

As an application end user, we are giving our microservices-based end users an application URL they can hit to view negative tweets on a monitored Twitter handle, along with their scores against social tone. For this application to function as intended, we need our microservice 1 to be running, microservice 2 to be running, and eventually, to achieve any added value or extended functionality independent of microservices 1 and 2, we need our microservices 3 to be available and running. In the current scenario, microservice 3 does not add value to the existing use case, but it nevertheless provides a handle to implement any function without having to edit or update microservices 1 and 2. Follow the steps given here to see the results:

1. Go to a browser and hit the application URL, which is
   `https://analyse-twitemotion-b05307.mybluemix.net/translatedtwe ets` in this case.

2. You will see a response on your browser, as shown in the following screenshot:

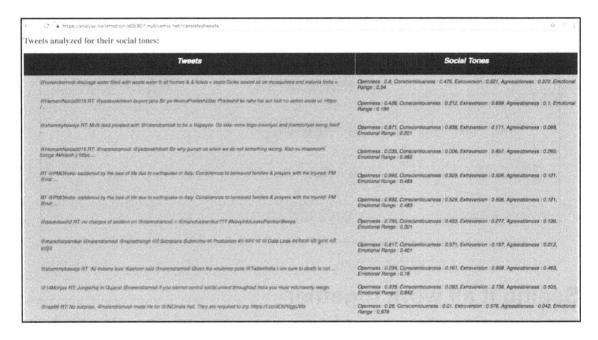

3. Go to your Bluemix dashboard and navigate to OpenWhisk dashboard. You will see the activity log indicating the execution of your OpenWhisk action, triggered by microservice 2 triggering your `B05307_07_CloudantTrigger` trigger:

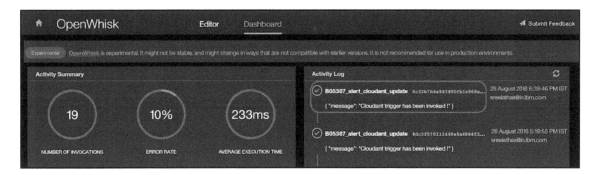

This completes the illustration of microservices-based application development on Bluemix.

Summary

In this chapter, you learned about the microservices architecture pattern. You should now be able to differentiate between a monolithic application and an application that is composed of microservices. You also learned about how Bluemix, as a cloud platform, provides the ability to seamlessly develop microservices-based applications. Going a step further, you can attempt to configure scaling policies on each of the applications separately and see it perform. Also, you will note that a failure to any one microservice does not bring down the other microservices. You can explore further and build various interesting and innovative microservices-based applications on Bluemix by leveraging the value-added services that Bluemix offers.

In the next chapter, we will look at another exciting set of services on Bluemix, these are services in **Mobile** category, which help with mobile application development.

10
Mobile Application Development on Bluemix

In the previous chapter we learnt about the architecture pattern for application development on cloud, called Microservices architecture pattern. We also learnt how to use Bluemix and services on Bluemix to build and deploy applications that employ the microservices architecture.

In this chapter, we will learn to develop a simple mobile client application using Bluemix, and we will also learn the use of Bluemix services with the mobile applications. You will also see how easy it is to get started with your mobile application development using the template applications provided out of the box in the mobile dashboard on Bluemix.

 Discussions in this chapter will be based upon the capabilities that are available on Bluemix at the time of writing this book.

In this chapter, we will be covering the following topics:

- Learn about the mobile category services available on Bluemix
- Create a mobile application using the mobile dashboard on Bluemix
- Integrate the Push Notifications service to your mobile application
- Send push notifications to your mobile application and see it all working together

Mobile category services

Services under the **Mobile** category, as seen in the Bluemix catalog, are as follows:

- **Mobile Analytics**: This is an IBM service
- **Mobile Application Content Manager**: This is an IBM service
- **Mobile Client Access**: This is an IBM service
- **Mobile Foundation**: This is an IBM service
- **Push Notifications**: This is an IBM service
- **Mobile Quality Assurance**: This is an IBM service
- **TestdroidCloud**: This is a third-party service
- **Twilio**: This is a third-party service
- **Kinetise**: This is a third-party service

When you log in to Bluemix and select the **Mobile** category, you will be taken to what is known as the Mobile Dashboard:

From here you can create a new mobile project, or you can add a mobile service instance by clicking the **Get started now!** icon in the top-right corner, as shown in the following screenshot:

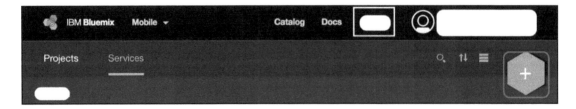

Clicking the **Get started now!** icon will display the mobile services available on Bluemix. At the time of writing this book, the available mobile services are as shown in the following screenshot:

An in-depth description of these services is outside the scope of this book.

 To learn more about each of these mobile services, refer to `https://ibm.b iz/Bdrbmc`.

Let us look at how to create a simple mobile application and how we can configure the application to use some of the services provided by Bluemix.

Creating a mobile application

In this section, we will learn how to create a new mobile project on Bluemix and how to modify it to suit your requirements. Later in this section, you will also learn how we can configure the mobile service **Push Notifications** to send notifications to a mobile device running the application.

Creating a mobile project

Once you have logged into the Bluemix organization and space where you want to create the mobile application, you can follow the steps given here to create the new mobile application:

1. From the mobile dashboard, **Projects**, click on **New Project** to start creating your mobile project:

2. There will be options for the type of application you want to create; based on the choice made, a template or starter application will be created for you. By default the **Empty App** template is selected. For our discussion in this chapter, we will be creating a catalog application. Therefore, as shown in the following screenshot, choose **Store Catalog** and click **Create**:

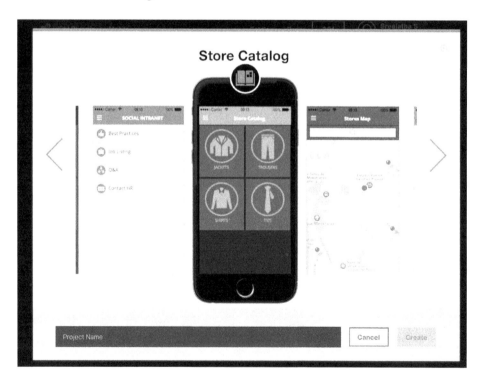

3. Once the application is created, you can edit it to suit your application requirements. For our demonstration, we will be creating a store catalog for beauty products.

> Similarly, you can modify this application to create a catalog for any category of products or services.

4. Once you open the project in edit mode, you can see the various levers you can work with, as shown in the following screenshot:

5. To modify the UI or UX of the application, we will use the **Design** function, with which you will be able to modify how your application looks and behaves. The following screenshot shows what you will see for the catalog application you just created. You will notice that each of the existing screens can be modified from here, and you can also add new screens to your application:

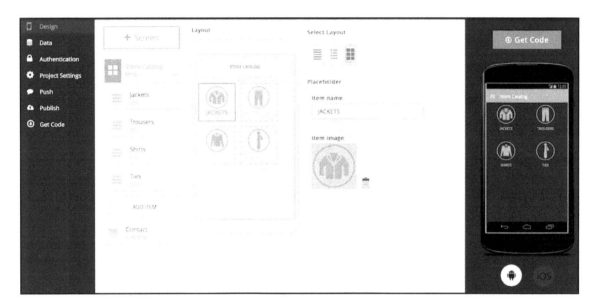

6. We will use the **Data** option to build the data store for your application. Given that we are building a store catalog for beauty products, we should modify and add content to the data store from here, so that we populate it with the required products and product details. The following screenshot shows what you will see for the catalog application you just created. You will notice that you can edit the existing rows, add new rows, or remove existing rows from here:

7. To change the catalog application to an application that catalogs beauty products, go ahead and make changes to the **Design** and **Data** sections of your mobile project. The following screenshot shows the sample data populated for beauty products; you can manually add content relevant to your application:

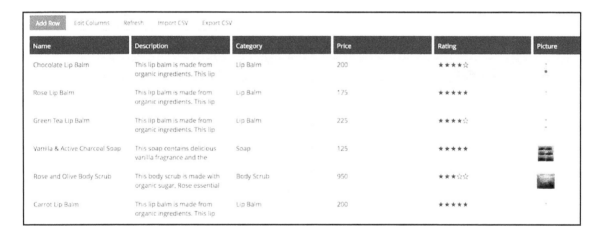

8. You can make changes to the screen names and other details on your application screens using the **Design** editor. The modified screens for the beauty product catalog used for this demonstration are as shown in the following screenshot:

 Note that we have not discussed the detailed steps to make modifications to the catalog application here; this is left to your own creativity. The **Design** editor is intuitive and will guide you through making the changes that you would want.

9. In **Project Settings**, you can further define how your application appears in terms of the colors used for text, action bar, background, and so on. You can also see your application **Bundle Identifier** and upload a logo for your application here:

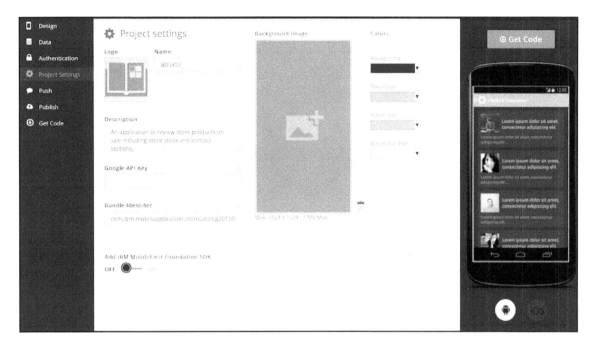

10. You will also notice that you can add **IBM MobileFirst Foundation SDK** to your application and leverage the capabilities provided by the Foundation platform within your application. If you already have a licensed version of the IBM MobileFirst Foundation product, you can also use the **Mobile Foundation** service on Bluemix:

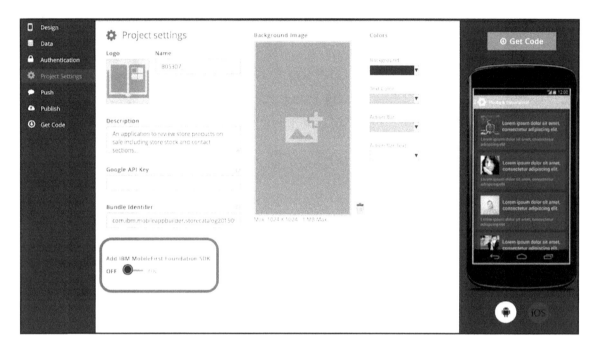

To learn more about the **Mobile Foundation** service and how to use it, refer to `https://ibm.biz/Bdrban`.

11. Once you are sure that you have made the application changes necessary to build your own catalog, in this case the catalog for beauty products, then you can go to **Get Code** and download the source code and the application bundle or apk based on the OS you want to use to run your application:

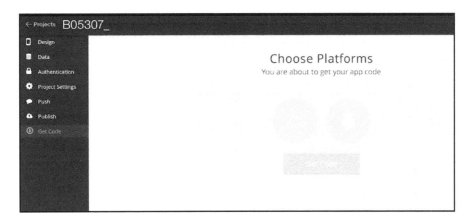

12. For this demonstration we will be using the Android platform. Select Android, as shown in the following screenshot:

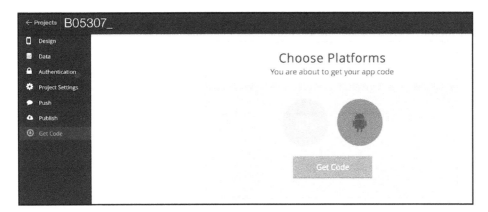

13. Click **Get Code**. You will see that your application code is being generated:

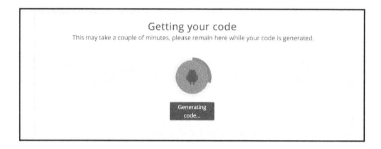

14. You will see that this also compiles the application code:

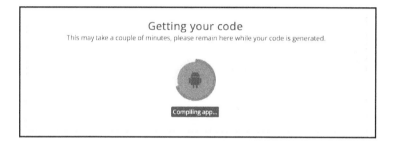

15. Once this completes, you can see that you are provided with options to download the source code for your application or the APK file, since the platform we selected was Android. You can also try the application on your Android device by using the **Try it!** option, as shown in the following screenshot:

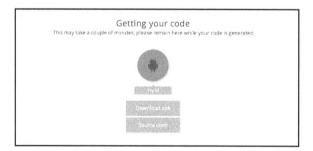

16. Click **Try it!** and you will see a QR code for your application, which can be scanned using an Android device. You can then see your catalog application running on your device:

17. As shown in the screenshot of Step 15, click **Download apk** to download the apk for your application. You can use any Android device to launch your application by copying this apk to the device. Click **Source code** to download the source code for your application. The source code is required if you would like to further modify your application source and rebuild it before running it on a device. You will see the following structure for the downloaded apk and source code files:

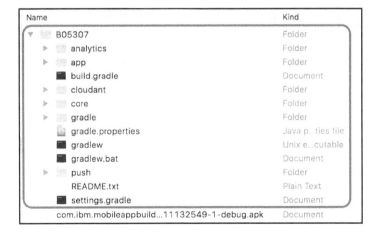

Running the application on an Android emulator

In this section, we will learn how to run the application you just created in an Android emulator using Android Studio.

You can download the latest version of Android Studio for your OS from `https://developer.android.com/studio/index.html`. For instructions on how to install and work with Android Studio, refer to `https://developer.android.com/studio/install.html`.

Assuming you have installed Android Studio, follow the instructions given here to work with the application code that you downloaded in the previous section:

1. Click **File** | **Open** from the menu in Android Studio, as shown in the following screenshot:

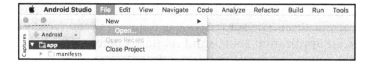

2. Browse to the source code folder you downloaded in the previous section. Choose the project folder, which is `B05307` in this demo. Once the studio opens the mobile project, you will see the following resources and structure in your studio window:

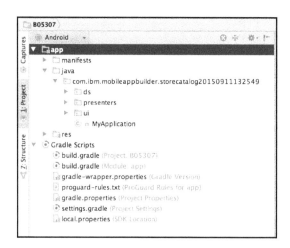

3. To run the application, click the play icon, as shown in the following screenshot:

4. You will be prompted to select the emulator type and launch it, as shown in the following screenshot:

5. If you do not find the desired virtual device type, you can click the highlighted button and create the virtual device you want to use. Click the highlighted button shown in the preceding screenshot; this will open the dialog shown in the following screenshot, where you can click **Create Virtual Device** to create the virtual device with the chosen target API version and architecture. You can then select this device and launch the emulator:

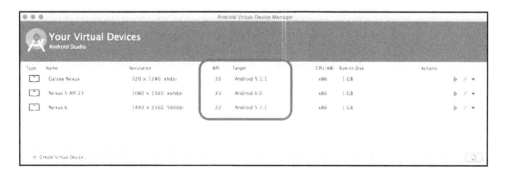

6. The emulator launches your application and you will see the application on the emulated device. The welcome or start page for your application is displayed in the following screenshot:

7. Clicking **Lip Balms** on the app will open the lip balm variants available in the store, as designed previously:

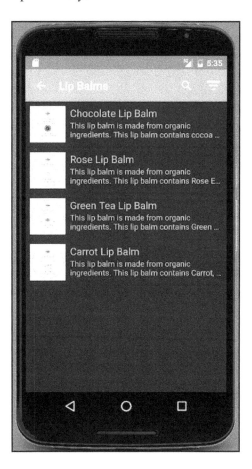

8. You can view the details of each of the products by clicking on the individual product; the details page will be displayed, as shown in the following screenshot:

9. Similarly, you can view the other available products from the list, such as **Body Scrubs**, as shown in the following screenshot:

10. The details page for **Rose and Olive Body Scrub** is as shown in the following screenshot:

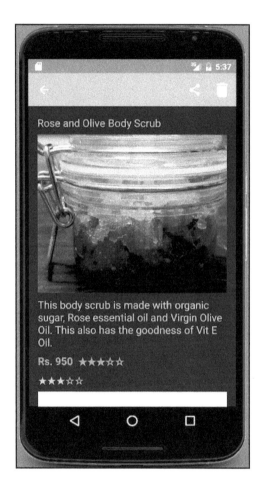

Integrating Push Notifications to the application

In the previous section, we learned how to create a mobile application from a template, how to customize it, and how to download it and work with it on your local Android Studio. In this section, we will learn how to extend your mobile application so that it can receive push notifications from the server.

Push Notifications is an asynchronous way of sending messages to application users' devices. To enable this, we will use the Push Notifications service on Bluemix.

Creating the Push Notifications service instance

Let us first create the Push Notifications service instance. Follow the steps given here to create the service instance:

1. Log in to Bluemix, and select the **Mobile** category to go to the Mobile dashboard:

2. From here you can add a mobile service instance by clicking the **Get started now!** icon in the top-right corner, as shown in the following screenshot:

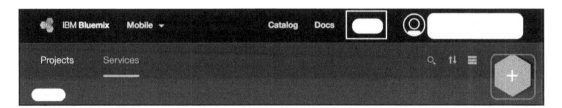

3. Clicking the **Get started now!** icon will display the mobile services available on Bluemix. Select **Push Notifications**:

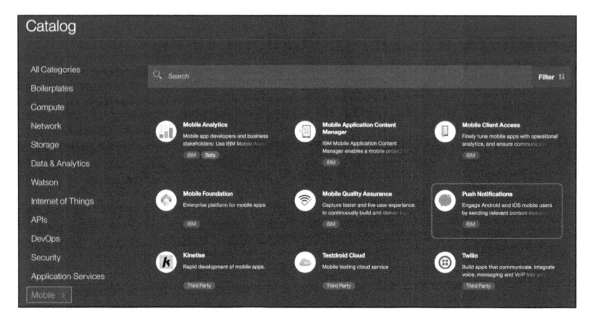

4. Review the details of the service, select the **Basic** service plan, and click **Create**:

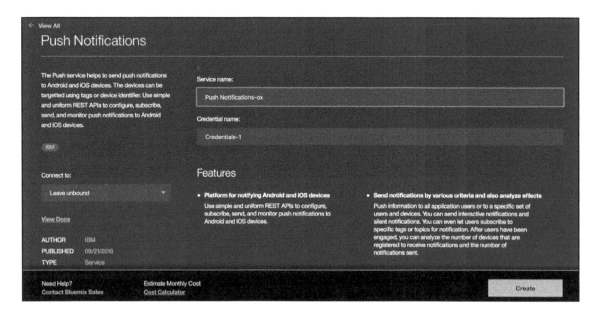

5. The service instance created is displayed in the Mobile dashboard under the **Services** tab, as shown in the following screenshot:

Next let us configure the Push Notifications service instance.

Configuring the Push Notifications service instance

In this section, we will see how we should configure the Push Notifications service instance so that it can be used to send notifications to your catalog application. Follow the steps given here to configure your Push Notifications service instance:

1. From under the **Services** tab in the Mobile dashboard, click the Push Notifications service instance we created:

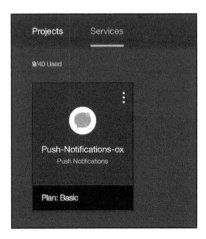

2. Go to the **Configure** section, as shown in the following screenshot. Here you will see a button called **Mobile Options**:

3. Click **Mobile Options**. You will see the details required to configure your application to integrate to this Push Notifications service instance. Make a note of the **App Route** and the **App GUID** fields, as shown in the following screenshot:

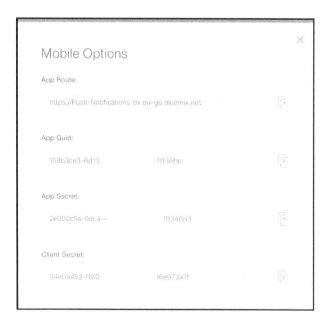

4. Further below on the **Configure** screen, you will need to configure GCM (Google Cloud Messaging) credentials. Since our application is an Android app we will be using GCM as the asynchronous messaging service provider.

To read further on GCM, refer to
`https://developers.google.com/cloud-messaging/`.

5. You will first need to create a GoogleAPI project and enable API on it. You will then need to create a Server Key. For more details about how to do this, refer to `https://ibm.biz/Bdr8VK`.

6. Once you have the sender ID and API key available for your GoogleAPI project, you can continue with the configuration of your Push Notifications service instance. Update the **Sender ID** and **API Key** created under the GCM credentials in your Push Notifications service, as shown in the following screenshot:

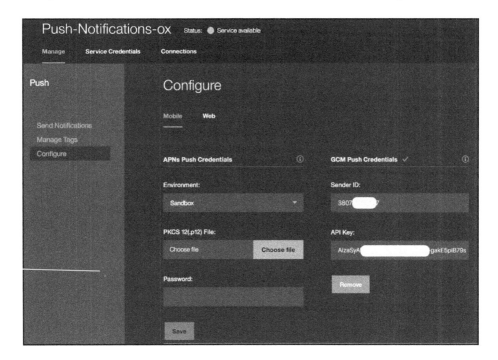

This completes the configuration of the Push Notifications service. Let us now learn how to integrate the Push Notifications service instance with the application.

Integrating the Push Notifications service with an application

Go back to the Mobile dashboard and follow the steps given here:

1. From under the **Projects** tab, select **Edit** on the store catalog application we created earlier in this chapter:

2. In the application edit view, go to the **Push** section. For the option to **Enable notifications for this project**, pull the slider to **ON**, as shown in the following screenshot:

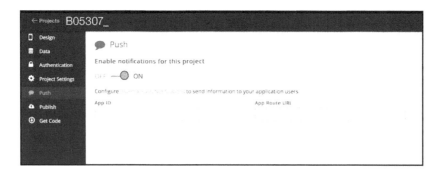

3. Next you will need to configure the **App ID** and **App Route URL** fields; this information was obtained when we configured the Push Notifications service instance in the previous section, under the **Mobile Options** of your Push Notifications **Configure** screen. Provide those values here, as shown in the following screenshot:

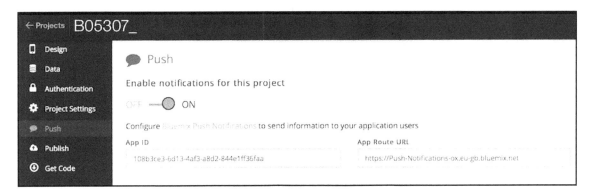

This completes the steps to integrate the Push Notifications service with your application. Let us now see them work together.

Sending Push Notifications to your application

We will use the same method of testing this in Android Studio using an Android emulator. Follow the steps given here to see all of this working together:

1. You will need to download the source code again using the **Get Code** option we discussed previously:

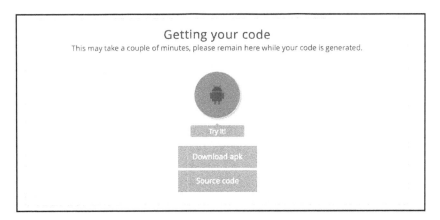

2. Open the downloaded source code in Android Studio using the steps described previously.

3. Once the project is opened, launch the app in a selected **AVD** (**Android Virtual Device**), which acts as the Android emulator. You will see the application launched as before, as shown in the following screenshot:

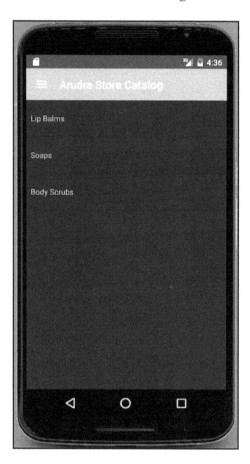

4. Now let's simulate the condition where the application distributors or the store owners want to inform their customers of certain updates or discounts via app notifications. For this we will go to the Push Notifications service instance from the mobile dashboard:

5. Click the service tile to open it and go to the **Send Notifications** section, as shown in the following screenshot:

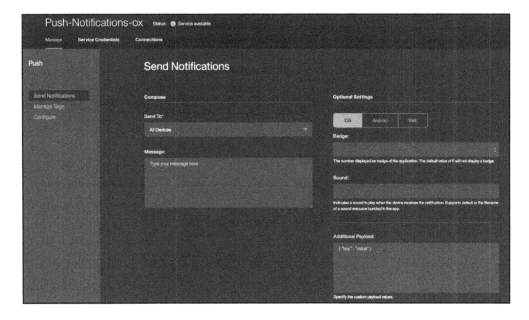

This is where you can type a notification message and send it to applications that have registered to receive notifications, in other words, apps that are installed on host devices.

Notifications can be sent based on device operating systems, tags subscribed to, and so on. For the sake of simplicity, here we will demonstrate this feature with **Send To** selected and retaining the default value of **All Devices**. For more information on tag-based authentication, refer to `https://ibm.biz/Bdr8J3`.

6. Let's now type two separate notification messages and send them to all devices where the app is installed. Two notification messages are shown in the following screenshots:

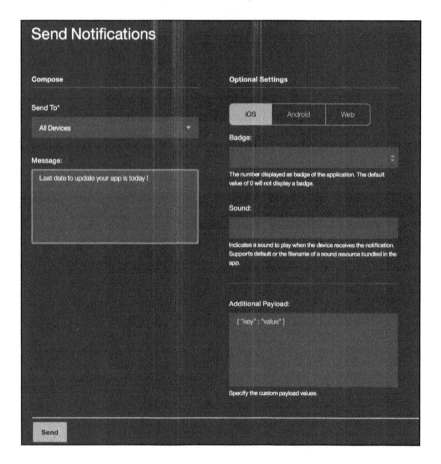

7. Click **SEND**. Now type the next notification message, as shown in the following screenshot:

8. Click **SEND**. You will see the success message on the screen, as shown in the following screenshot, if the notifications were successfully sent out from the Push Notifications service:

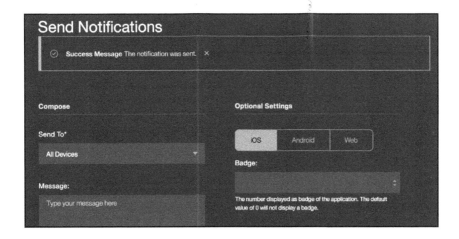

9. Let's now go back to the Android emulator we launched our application with in Step 3 of this section. You will now see two stars appearing in the notification tray, as shown in the following screenshot:

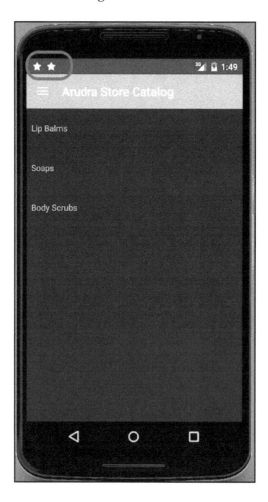

10. You can click on the notification alerts to see the notification details, as shown in the following screenshot:

So, with this we learned how to configure your mobile application to use the Push Notifications service on Bluemix, to receive app notifications. Next let us learn how to modify the application code to format the notification message display:

1. To format your notification view, you will need to modify the StoreCatalogScreen1Fragment class in your source code. This is where you will implement the MFPPushNotificationListener interface. The modified StoreCatalogScreen1Fragment class would be as follows:

```
package com.ibm.mobileappbuilder.storecatalog20150911132549.ui;
import android.app.AlertDialog;
import android.content.Context;
import android.content.DialogInterface;
import android.os.Bundle;
```

```
import android.util.Log;
import com.ibm.mobileappbuilder.storecatalog20150911132549.R;
import com.ibm.mobilefirstplatform.clientsdk.android.push.
  api.MFPPush;
import com.ibm.mobilefirstplatform.clientsdk.android.push.
  api.MFPPushNotificationListener;
import com.ibm.mobilefirstplatform.clientsdk.android.push.api.
  MFPSimplePushNotification;
import java.util.ArrayList;
import java.util.List;
import ibmmobileappbuilder.MenuItem;
import ibmmobileappbuilder.actions.StartActivityAction;
import ibmmobileappbuilder.util.Constants;
/**
 * StoreCatalogScreen1Fragment menu fragment.
 */public class StoreCatalogScreen1Fragment extends
  ibmmobileappbuilder.ui.MenuFragment implements
  MFPPushNotificationListener{
    private MFPPush push = null;
    private Context _this;
    private static final String TAG = "StoreCatalogScreen1Frag";/**
 * Default constructor
 */
public StoreCatalogScreen1Fragment(){
  super();
}
// Factory method
public static StoreCatalogScreen1Fragment newInstance(Bundle args) {
  StoreCatalogScreen1Fragment fragment = new
    StoreCatalogScreen1Fragment();
  fragment.setArguments(args);
  return fragment;
}
@Override
public void onCreate(Bundle savedInstanceState) {
  super.onCreate(savedInstanceState);
  _this = getActivity();
  // MFPPush is initialized in PushNotificationsApplication.class
  push = MFPPush.getInstance();
  // Option for receiving push notifications
  push.listen(this);
}
// Menu Fragment interface
@Override
public List<MenuItem>getMenuItems() {
  ArrayList<MenuItem> items = new ArrayList<MenuItem>();
  items.add(new MenuItem()
    .setLabel("Lip Balms")
```

```
      .setIcon(R.drawable.jpg_lbgreentea353)
      .setAction(new StartActivityAction(LipBalmsActivity.class,
        Constants.DETAIL))
  );
  items.add(new MenuItem()
    .setLabel("Soaps")
    .setIcon(R.drawable.png_soaps511)
    .setAction(new StartActivityAction(SoapsActivity.class,
      Constants.DETAIL))
  );
  items.add(new MenuItem()
    .setLabel("Body Scrubs")
    Icon(R.drawable.png_screenshot20160816at11825pm255)
    .setAction(new StartActivityAction(BodyScrubsActivity.class,
      Constants.DETAIL))
  );
  return items;
}
@Override
public intgetLayout() {
  return R.layout.fragment_list;
}
@Override
public intgetItemLayout() {
  return R.layout.storecatalogscreen1_item;
}
@Override
public void onPause() {
  super.onPause();
  if (push != null) {
    push.hold();
  }
}
@Override
public void onResume() {
  super.onResume();
  if (push != null) {
    push.listen(this);
  }
}
public void showAlertMsg(final String title, final String msg) {
  Runnable run = new Runnable() {
    @Override
    public void run() {
      // Create an AlertDialog Builder, and configure alert
      AlertDialog.Builder builder = new
        AlertDialog.Builder(_this);
      builder.setTitle(title)
```

```
    .setMessage(msg)
    .setPositiveButton("Okay",
      new DialogInterface.OnClickListener() {
      @Override
      public void onClick(DialogInterface dialog, int which) {
        Log.i(TAG, "Okay was pressed");
      }
    });
    // Create the AlertDialog
    AlertDialog dialog = builder.create();
    // Display the dialog
    dialog.show();
    }
  };
  getActivity().runOnUiThread(run);
}
@Override public void
  onReceive(MFPSimplePushNotificationmfpSimplePushNotification) {
  Log.i("Push Notifications", mfpSimplePushNotification.getAlert());
  String alert = "" + mfpSimplePushNotification.getAlert();
  showAlertMsg("Arudra Store Catalog", alert);
}
```

2. You will need to rebuild and relaunch your application in Android Studio. Your updated application is launched, as shown in the following screenshot:

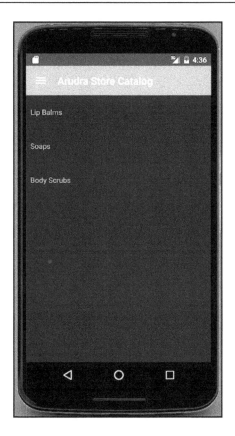

3. Let us go back to the Push Notifications service, the **Send Notifications** screen. Type the notification message shown in the following screenshot and click **SEND**:

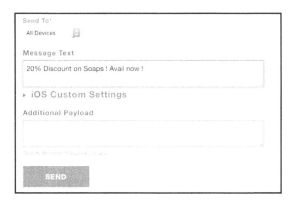

4. Go back to the application you launched in Step 2 of this section. You will now see the notification displayed as an alert. This is due to the changes we made to the way notification views should be created in the `StoreCatalogScreen1Fragment` class:

With this, we learned how to modify the Android application in Android Studio. We also learned how to customize how the push notification message should appear to the application user, on their device. Until now we have been sending notification messages to the application using the Push Notifications service instance UI on Bluemix. Alternatively, we can use REST APIs to send notification messages to client applications. This method is largely useful when you want to automate the process of sending notifications triggered by some backend activity. Let us take a quick look at the use of REST APIs to send a notification message to the store catalog application.

You will need a REST client to perform the next set of steps. You can use any commercially available REST client. For this demonstration, we are using Postman, which is a Chrome browser extension.

 You can download Postman from `http://bit.ly/1HCOCwF`.

 Before you start working with REST APIs, it is recommended that you understand the API syntax and samples by going through the API documentation at `https://ibm.biz/Bdr5Ku` and `https://ibm.biz/Bdr5K9`.

To learn how to send push notifications using REST APIs, carry out the following steps:

1. Open your REST client and type the complete URL that is used to send a notification; use the URL format shown in the following screenshot. You can replace the App ID in the URI with your own App ID. Also, make sure your Push Notifications service is available on Bluemix, the region is specified in the URL domain, and configure the **Headers** section as shown in the following screenshot:

2. To get the **App Secret** key, go to **Service Credentials** in your Push Notifications service instance, as shown in the following screenshot:

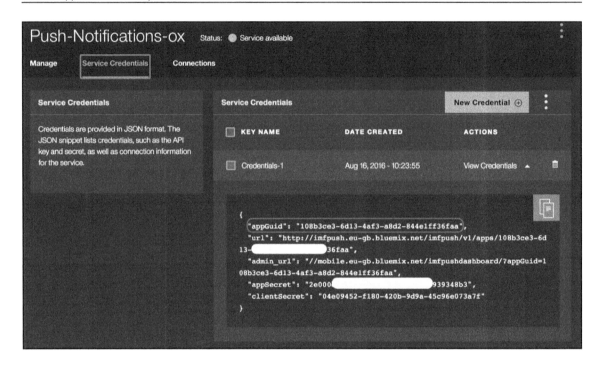

3. In the REST client, once you have configured the **Headers** section, go to the **Body** section; here you can paste the following message JSON as the request body. Note that we have not specified any device IDs in the request JSON, which means that this notification will be sent to all devices registered to receive notifications for this application:

```
{
  "message": {
    "alert": "Grab your discount of 10% on all products !",
  },
  "target": {
    "deviceIds": [],
    "platforms": ["G"],
    "tagNames": [],
    "userIds": ["anonymous"]
  }
}
```

 To learn more about the request message syntax, refer to
https://ibm.biz/Bdr8AT.

4. Make sure the URL is correct and that the HTTP method is POST. Click **Send**.

5. You will see the response for a successful send of the notification message, as shown in the following screenshot:

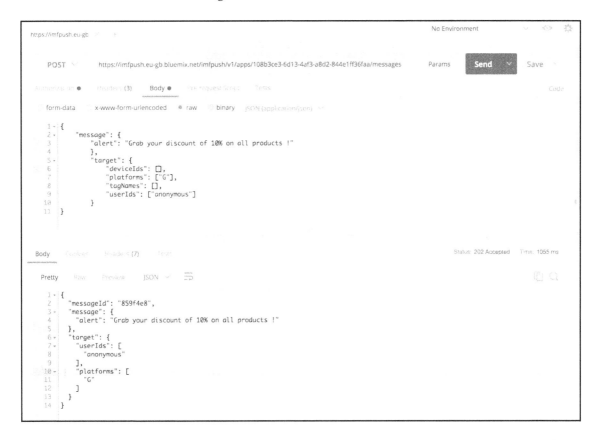

6. Go back to the application you have launched using Android Studio. You will see the notification received, as shown in the following screenshot:

Next let us see how to use the same API method to send a notification to a specific device.

For details on the API syntax and samples, go through the API documentation at `https://ibm.biz/Bdr5K9`.

For this we will need to do one additional step, which is to find the device IDs for the devices that are registered to receive push notifications. For this, execute the REST API to GET the devices registered:

1. In the REST client, once you have configured the **Headers** section, make sure the URL is correct and that the HTTP method is `GET`. Click **Send**.

2. You will see the response for a successful GET, as shown in the following screenshot. You can see the device IDs returned as a response to the GET request:

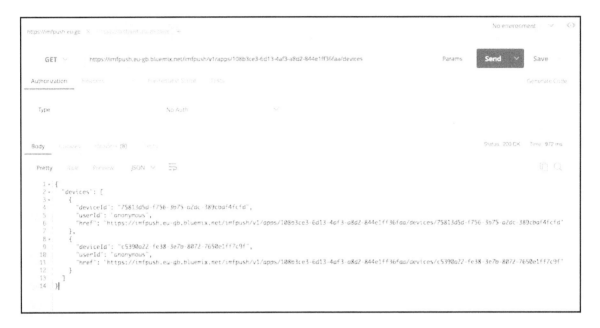

3. Now, using the same REST client, change your URL to the one that is used to send push notifications. Use the following code in the request JSON message; you will notice that this time, the device ID is specified to be one of the values we got by executing the API to retrieve the devices that are registered:

```
{
  "message": {
    "alert": "Grab your discount of 10% on all products !",
  },
  "target": {
    "deviceIds": [75813d5d-f756-3b75-a2dc-389cbaf4fcfd],
    "platforms": ["G"],
    "tagNames": [],
    "userIds": ["anonymous"]
  }
}
```

4. Make sure the URL is correct and that the HTTP method is POST. Click **Send**.

5. You will see the response for a successful send of the notification message, as shown in the following screenshot:

6. Go back to the application you have launched using Android Studio. You will see the notification received, as shown in the following screenshot:

With this, we have also learned how to work with REST APIs to send push notifications to your mobile client application.

Summary

In this chapter, we learned how we can easily develop, customize, and extend a mobile application using the capabilities on Bluemix. We also learned how to use one of the value-added mobile services on Bluemix, Push Notifications, and how to use it with your application. You also learned how to extend your mobile application locally to build features or value into the application after starting from a quick starter or template application, provided on Bluemix.

With this chapter, you have completed the basics of the IBM Bluemix cloud platform. If you have followed the steps to work with Bluemix as discussed in each of the chapters in this book, then you are equipped to begin your journey to explore further and to discover the other powerful and useful services and capabilities of the Bluemix platform. This book is an attempt to introduce you to Bluemix and to enable you to get your hands dirty. You have now scratched the surface, go ahead and dive deep. Discover the power of Bluemix platform as a service and what it has to offer to define the applications and workloads of the future. Experience the convergence of path defining technologies such as cognitive (Watson), Internet of Things, Mobile, and DevOps to name a few, on a single platform, IBM Bluemix.

It is time to sign off; we are concluding this book with the belief that we have got you started well on your cloud journey, with this book. We recommend you continue the process of learning and leverage your learnings to define technology and business.

Index